Quantum Compu

Computing And Humanity's Next Frontier

Dr Alex Bugeja, PhD

Table of Contents

Introduction

Take a moment to look around you. Chances are, you are surrounded by the quiet hum of computation. It's in the smartphone in your pocket, the laptop on your desk, the smart television on your wall, and even the thermostat regulating the temperature of your room. In the span of a single human lifetime, we have journeyed from room-sized machines clattering away at simple arithmetic to globally interconnected devices that hold the sum of human knowledge. This digital revolution, silent and relentless, has been powered by a simple yet profound concept: the bit. A bit is the most basic unit of information in classical computing, a humble switch that can be in one of two states: on or off, represented by a 1 or a 0. Every email you send, every photo you take, every movie you stream is, at its core, an unimaginably vast sequence of these simple ones and zeros.

For decades, our ability to cram more and more of these tiny switches onto microchips has followed a predictable and explosive trajectory known as Moore's Law. This observation, which predicted the number of transistors on a chip would double approximately every two years, has been the engine of technological progress. It's the reason the phone you hold in your hand is millions of times more powerful than the computers that guided the Apollo missions to the moon. We have become masters of the bit, manipulating these ones and zeros with incredible speed and precision to build the modern world. However, this relentless march of progress is beginning to encounter a formidable barrier: the laws of physics themselves. As we shrink our transistors down to the scale of just a few atoms, we are entering a realm where the familiar rules of the classical world begin to break down.

It turns out there are entire classes of problems that are fundamentally beyond the reach of even the most powerful supercomputers we can envision. These are not problems that we can solve by simply building bigger or faster classical computers. The complexity of these challenges grows at a rate so astronomical that even a computer the size of the known universe, running for the entire age of the universe, couldn't crack them. Imagine trying to design a new life-saving drug. To do so, you need to understand precisely how a candidate molecule will interact with complex proteins in the human body. The number of possible configurations and interactions is staggering, far too vast for a classical computer, which must check each possibility one by one, to simulate accurately.

Or consider the challenge of creating new materials with desirable properties, such as a superconductor that works at room temperature, which would revolutionize energy transmission. The behavior of the electrons in these materials is governed by the strange laws of the quantum world, and simulating that behavior is a task that overwhelms classical computation. We face similar intractable problems in optimizing global logistics, designing new catalysts to combat climate change, and breaking the sophisticated encryption that protects our digital infrastructure. Our classical computers, for all their power, are like trying to solve a complex, multi-dimensional puzzle using only a simple on-off switch. They are powerful tools, but they speak the wrong language to describe the universe at its most fundamental level.

This is where our story begins. What if, instead of fighting against the strange and counter-intuitive rules of the microscopic world, we embraced them? What if we could build a new kind of computer, one that operates not on the simple binary logic of bits, but on the rich, complex, and frankly bizarre principles of quantum mechanics? This is the central promise of quantum computing: a complete reimagining of what a computer is and what it can do. It's not simply the next step on the ladder of technological progress; it's a leap onto an entirely new ladder. A quantum computer is not just a faster classical computer, any more than a light bulb is just a faster candle. It is a fundamentally different tool, designed to solve a fundamentally different class of problems.

To understand this new frontier, we must venture into a realm that defies our everyday intuition. It's a world where particles can be in multiple places at once, a concept known as superposition. Think of a spinning coin before it lands. While it's in the air, it is neither heads nor tails; in a sense, it is both simultaneously. A quantum bit, or "qubit," can exist in a similar state, representing both a 0 and a 1 at the same time. This ability to explore a vast number of possibilities at once is one of the foundational sources of a quantum computer's power.

Then there is entanglement, a phenomenon so strange that Albert Einstein famously dismissed it as "spooky action at a distance." When two qubits become entangled, their fates are intertwined, no matter how far apart they are. If you measure the state of one, you instantly know the state of the other, as if they are communicating faster than the speed of light. This profound interconnectedness allows for powerful computational shortcuts and correlations that are impossible in the classical world. It's a resource as fundamental as energy, one that we are only now learning to harness.

These concepts—superposition and entanglement—are not just philosophical curiosities. They are the working cogs of a quantum computer. By manipulating qubits that are in superpositions of states and entangled with one another, a quantum computer can explore a problem's entire landscape of potential solutions simultaneously. Where a classical computer would have to trudge through every possible path one by one, a quantum computer can survey all paths at once, quickly homing in on the correct answer. This inherent parallelism is what will allow quantum machines to solve those currently unsolvable problems in medicine, materials science, and beyond.

So, why should you, a beginner in this field, care about this seemingly esoteric technology? Because the impact of quantum computing is poised to be revolutionary, touching nearly every aspect of our lives. In medicine, quantum computers will allow us to simulate molecules with perfect accuracy, leading to the rapid design of new drugs and personalized therapies tailored to an individual's genetic makeup. It could take the development of new medicines from a decade-long process of trial and error to a targeted, efficient simulation.

In the world of finance, quantum algorithms will be able to optimize investment strategies and model economic risks with a level of sophistication that is currently unimaginable. For manufacturing and logistics, they promise to solve incredibly complex optimization problems, finding the most efficient shipping routes, streamlining factory operations, and designing more resilient supply chains. And in the fight against climate change, quantum computing could be a game-changer, helping us discover new catalysts for carbon capture, design more efficient solar cells, and create better batteries for storing renewable energy.

The quantum revolution also brings with it a profound challenge to our digital security. The encryption methods that protect everything from our bank accounts to government secrets rely on the fact that it is incredibly difficult for classical computers to factor large numbers. For a quantum computer, however, this task is trivial. A sufficiently powerful quantum machine could shatter much of the cryptography that underpins our modern world. This presents both a threat and an opportunity, spurring the development of new, "quantum-resistant" cryptographic methods to secure our information in this new era.

This book is your guide to this new and exciting frontier. It is written for the curious, for the beginner who has heard the buzz about quantum computing but has been intimidated by the seemingly impenetrable science behind it. You do not need an advanced degree in physics or mathematics to join this journey. Our goal is to demystify the core concepts of quantum computing, to strip away the intimidating jargon and present the foundational ideas in a clear, straightforward, and engaging way. We will rely on analogies and thought experiments rather than dense equations, building your understanding one concept at a time.

We will begin our exploration by diving into the dawn of this new computing era, understanding the limitations of classical computers that created the need for a new paradigm. From there, we will journey into the quantum realm itself, exploring the strange and wonderful principles that govern the world of the very small. You will meet the star of the show, the qubit, and learn how its unique properties of superposition and entanglement give quantum computers their power.

With these building blocks in hand, we will see how they are assembled into quantum gates and circuits, the quantum equivalent of the logic gates that power our classical devices. We will then explore the "killer apps" of the quantum world: the groundbreaking algorithms, like Shor's for factoring and Grover's for searching, that promise to solve problems once thought impossible.

Our journey will then take us from the theoretical to the practical. We will look under the hood at the incredible hardware being developed to build these machines, from trapped ions and superconducting circuits to photons. We will confront the immense challenges that researchers face, primarily the problem of "noise" and decoherence, and the clever error-correction techniques being designed to tame the fragile quantum world.

Finally, we will survey the landscape of the quantum age, exploring the real-world applications that are already on the horizon. We will discuss quantum's impact on cryptography, scientific simulation, and the future of artificial intelligence through quantum machine learning. We will consider the economic and ethical implications of this transformative technology and provide a roadmap for how you can continue your own learning and even get involved in the quantum community. This book is an invitation to be a part of the next great technological leap forward, to understand the principles that will shape the twenty-first century and beyond. The quantum frontier awaits.

CHAPTER ONE: The Dawn of a New Computing Era

Every great revolution has its defining rhythm, a steady beat of progress that seems, for a time, unstoppable. For the digital age, that rhythm was set by Moore's Law. It wasn't a law of nature, like gravity, but rather a remarkably prescient observation made in 1965 by Gordon Moore, the co-founder of Intel. He predicted that the number of transistors one could cram onto an integrated circuit would double roughly every two years. This exponential growth became the driving force of the modern world, a self-fulfilling prophecy that pushed engineers to innovate and companies to invest, all marching to the same relentless drumbeat. The result was an explosion of computational power that has transformed society in ways that would have been unimaginable just a few generations ago.

The pocket calculator that replaced the slide rule, the personal computer that brought the office into the home, the smartphone that put the entire internet in our hands—all are direct descendants of this incredible shrinking act. Each new generation of microchips, smaller, faster, and cheaper than the last, unlocked new possibilities. We learned to sequence the human genome, to build vast global communication networks, and to create artificially intelligent systems that can recognize faces, translate languages, and even compose music. We have been living through a golden age of classical computation, an era defined by the bit and powered by the ever-shrinking transistor.

However, no rhythm can last forever. The steady, predictable beat of Moore's Law is beginning to falter. The engine of progress is not so much running out of steam as it is running out of space. The miniaturization that has been the hallmark of the digital revolution is approaching a fundamental, physical barrier: the atomic scale. For decades, we have been playing a game of dimensional chess on a board made of silicon, and we are now down to the final, infinitesimally small squares. The era of easy, exponential gains is drawing to a close, and with its end comes a profound question: what comes next?

The primary challenge is that transistors, the fundamental switches of classical computers, are now so small that their components are measured in mere handfuls of atoms. As of 2022, IBM announced the development of a two-nanometer chip technology, a scale where a single silicon atom is about 0.2 nanometers. At this minuscule level, the predictable, classical laws of physics that govern a light switch or a water valve begin to give way to the strange and probabilistic rules of the quantum realm. The solid walls that keep the flow of electrons in check start to become unnervingly porous.

One of the most significant problems is a phenomenon known as quantum tunneling. Imagine throwing a tennis ball against a solid wall. In our everyday, classical world, the ball will always bounce back. It simply does not have enough energy to pass through. In the quantum world, however, there is a small but non-zero chance that the ball will simply appear on the other side of the wall, without ever breaking it. For an electron approaching a thin insulating barrier inside a transistor, this "tunneling" effect becomes a serious issue. The barrier is there to stop the flow of current when the transistor is in its "off" state, representing a 0. But as that barrier shrinks to just a few atoms thick, electrons can leak through, causing errors and wasting energy. Your "off" switch starts to flicker.

This electron leakage is not just a minor inconvenience; it contributes to one of the most stubborn problems in modern computing: heat. Every computation, every flip of a bit from 0 to 1 and back again, generates a tiny puff of waste heat. When you have billions of transistors switching billions of times per second on a chip the size of a fingernail, that tiny amount of heat adds up quickly. This thermal challenge has become a primary bottleneck. Processors have to be actively cooled, often with elaborate fans and heat sinks, and their maximum speed is often limited not by how fast they *can* go, but by how much heat can be safely drawn away before the chip begins to cook itself. Pushing for higher speeds by simply shrinking transistors further only exacerbates the problem, creating hotspots that can damage the chip and degrade performance.

So, the physical end of Moore's Law presents us with a formidable challenge. We can no longer rely on simply making things smaller to make them faster and more powerful. But even if we could somehow magically overcome these physical barriers, we would still face a more profound and fundamental limit. There exists a class of problems so monstrously complex that even a hypothetical, perfectly efficient classical computer the size of the galaxy would be powerless to solve them. These problems aren't limited by hardware, but by the very nature of computation itself.

To understand this, we need to touch upon the idea of computational complexity. Computer scientists often categorize problems based on how the time required to solve them scales with the size of the input. The "easy" problems belong to a class called P, for "Polynomial time." This means that as the problem gets bigger, the time it takes to solve it grows at a manageable, polynomial rate. Finding the largest number in a list is a P problem. If you double the length of the list, it might take you twice as long, but it doesn't become exponentially harder.

Then there is the class of "hard" problems, known as NP, for "Nondeterministic Polynomial time." A defining feature of these problems is that while finding a solution is incredibly difficult, verifying a potential solution is easy. For instance, if someone gives you the factors of a very large number, it is simple to multiply them together to check if they are correct. However, finding those factors in the first place is a different story altogether. The relationship between these two classes—whether P is equal to NP—is one of the most important unsolved questions in computer science and mathematics. The general consensus is that P does not equal NP, meaning there are problems for which verifying a solution is easy, but finding it is intractably hard.

The prime factorization of large numbers is the quintessential example of such a problem. A classical computer, at its core, must resort to a kind of brute-force method. It tries different combinations of numbers until it stumbles upon the correct factors. As the number of digits in the number to be factored increases, the number of potential combinations explodes at an exponential rate. This isn't just a matter of needing a slightly faster computer; the difficulty scales so dramatically that for numbers used in modern cryptography (which can have hundreds of digits), the time required to find the factors would be longer than the age of the universe.

Our entire digital security infrastructure is built upon this computational wall. When you send your credit card information over the internet, it is protected by encryption schemes like RSA, which rely on the practical impossibility for classical computers to factor large numbers. The security of global finance, government communications, and personal data all rests on the assumption that this is a problem our current machines simply cannot solve in any meaningful timeframe.

Factoring is just one example. Another famous hard problem is the "Traveling Salesman Problem." Imagine a salesperson who needs to visit a set of cities and wants to find the absolute shortest route that visits each city once before returning home. For a handful of cities, you could map out every possible route and pick the best one. But just like with factoring, the number of possible routes grows astronomically with each new city added. For just 30 cities, the number of possible routes is so vast that checking them all would take even the fastest supercomputers billions of years. This isn't an abstract puzzle; it's the heart of countless real-world optimization challenges in logistics, circuit design, and DNA sequencing.

The most profound limitation of classical computers, however, was articulated most clearly by the physicist Richard Feynman. In a keynote speech in 1981, he pointed to a challenge that cuts to the very heart of science. He observed that our world, at the most fundamental level of atoms and particles, is not classical—it is quantum mechanical. The rules that govern this realm are based on probability, uncertainty, and bizarre interactions that have no parallel in our everyday experience. Trying to simulate these quantum systems on a classical computer, which operates on the deterministic logic of 0s and 1s, is like trying to describe a symphony using only the words "loud" and "quiet."

Feynman argued that if you want to simulate a quantum system, you need a computer that itself operates on quantum principles. He famously declared, "Nature isn't classical, dammit, and if you want to make a simulation of Nature, you'd better make it quantum mechanical, and by golly it's a wonderful problem, because it doesn't look so easy." He envisioned a new kind of computer, one that could "think" in the native language of the universe. This would allow us to tackle problems far beyond the reach of any classical machine, such as accurately modeling the behavior of molecules for drug discovery, designing new materials with exotic properties, or unraveling the mysteries of high-energy physics.

These compounding challenges—the physical limits of silicon, the intractable nature of certain computational problems, and the inherent inability of classical machines to simulate the quantum world—have brought us to a critical juncture. The steady, reliable march of classical computing is slowing down, not because of a lack of ingenuity, but because we are pushing against the fundamental laws of physics and mathematics. The old paradigm, for all its spectacular success, has revealed its boundaries.

This realization is not a cause for despair, but for excitement. It signals the end of one chapter in the story of computation and the beginning of a new one. It marks the dawn of a new computing era, one that requires a radical departure from the binary logic that has served us so well. To solve the next generation of humanity's greatest challenges, we need more than just a faster horse; we need an entirely new mode of transportation. We must look beyond the bit and embrace the strange, powerful, and counter-intuitive logic of the quantum realm. The wall we have reached is not an end, but a doorway.

CHAPTER TWO: What Is Quantum? A Glimpse into the Quantum Realm

To step from the world of classical computing into the world of quantum computing is to cross a threshold into a new and bewildering country. The familiar landscape of cause and effect, of definite positions and predictable outcomes, gives way to a terrain governed by probability, uncertainty, and a logic that seems to actively defy common sense. Before we can hope to understand how a quantum computer works, we must first get a feel for this strange new territory. We must ask the fundamental question: what, exactly, is "quantum"? The word itself simply comes from the Latin for "how much," and it points to the single most important discovery that separates the quantum realm from our everyday world.

Imagine standing on a long, sloping ramp. In our classical, everyday experience, you can stand at any point along that ramp. You can move up or down by any amount, no matter how small. Your position is continuous. Now imagine that the ramp is replaced by a staircase. You can stand on the first step, or the second, or the third, but you can never stand one-and-a-half steps up. Your position is restricted to discrete, specific levels. This is the essential difference between the classical and quantum worlds. At the turn of the twentieth century, physicists discovered that the universe, at its most fundamental level, is a staircase, not a ramp.

This revolutionary idea was born not from a stroke of genius in a quiet study, but from a state of profound confusion. In the late 1800s, physicists were wrestling with a seemingly simple problem: how do hot objects glow? They were studying something called "black-body radiation," which is the light emitted by a perfect absorber and emitter of energy when it's heated. Think of a blacksmith's forge, where a piece of iron glows from dull red to orange to brilliant white as its temperature increases. Using the classical physics of the time, scientists tried to create a mathematical formula to predict the color and intensity of this glow. Their theories worked perfectly for the lower-energy, longer wavelengths of light (like red and infrared), but they failed spectacularly at the higher-energy, shorter wavelengths.

Their equations predicted that any hot object should be emitting an infinite amount of energy in the ultraviolet spectrum. This meant that even a warm teacup should be blasting out a lethal dose of high-energy radiation. This absurd conclusion was so at odds with reality that it was nicknamed the "ultraviolet catastrophe." Physics was broken, and no one knew how to fix it. The ramp of continuous energy, a foundational assumption of classical physics, was leading them off a cliff.

The solution came in 1900 from a German physicist named Max Planck. He proposed what he later called "an act of desperation." What if, he suggested, energy was not continuous? What if it could only be emitted or absorbed in discrete little packets, or "quanta"? He imagined the atoms in the hot object as tiny oscillators, and proposed that they couldn't just vibrate with any amount of energy. Instead, they could only hold energy in multiples of a fundamental unit, much like our staircase. An atom could have one unit of energy, or two, or three, but never two-and-a-half.

When Planck plugged this radical new assumption into the old equations, the ultraviolet catastrophe vanished. The math suddenly, and perfectly, described the observed glow of hot objects across the entire spectrum. By forcing energy to come in discrete chunks, his theory made it much harder for the object to emit high-energy ultraviolet light, as this would require saving up a very large and improbable "packet" of energy. Planck had stumbled upon a fundamental truth about the universe, almost by accident. He had discovered that energy is quantized, and in doing so, he had laid the first foundation stone of quantum mechanics.

Planck's idea was so strange that many, including Planck himself, were hesitant to accept its full implications. It was another five years before Albert Einstein took the next bold step. Einstein was contemplating a different puzzle, the "photoelectric effect." This is the phenomenon where shining a light on a piece of metal can knock electrons loose. Classical wave theory predicted that a brighter light (a more intense wave) should give the electrons more energy, knocking them out with greater speed. It also suggested that a very dim light, if you left it on long enough, should eventually build up enough energy to free an electron.

Experiments showed this was wrong. The energy of the ejected electrons depended not on the brightness of the light, but on its color (its frequency). A dim blue light could knock electrons out, while a very bright red light did nothing at all. And there was no time lag; if electrons were going to be freed, they were freed instantly. To explain this, Einstein took Planck's quantum idea and applied it to light itself. He proposed that light isn't a continuous wave, but is instead composed of a stream of tiny energy packets, which we now call photons.

Each photon carries a discrete amount of energy determined by its color. A photon of blue light has more energy than a photon of red light. An electron in the metal can only be knocked out if it gets hit by a single photon with enough energy to do the job. A thousand red-light photons hitting it are useless if none of them individually has the required energy. It's like trying to dislodge a coconut from a tree. You can throw a million ping-pong balls at it and nothing will happen. But one well-aimed baseball, with enough energy in a single packet, will do the trick. Einstein had shown that not just energy, but light itself, was quantized. The staircase model of the universe was becoming harder to ignore.

These discoveries revealed that the world of the very small is "grainy." But the true weirdness of the quantum realm was yet to come. The next revelation would shatter our most basic intuitions about the nature of reality itself, showing that particles can be in multiple places at once and that the very act of looking at something changes what you see. The key that unlocked this door was an elegantly simple piece of equipment: a barrier with two small, parallel slits cut into it.

This "double-slit experiment" is often described as the single most beautiful and baffling experiment in physics. To understand its profound implications, let's first consider how normal, classical objects would behave. Imagine you are firing a paintball gun at a wall with two slits in it. Behind the wall is a detector screen that records where each paintball hits. If you block the right slit, you'll get a single band of paint splatters on the screen, directly behind the left slit. If you block the left slit, you'll get a band behind the right one. If you open both slits, you'll simply get two overlapping bands of paint. Each paintball goes through one slit or the other and contributes to one of the two piles. Simple.

Now, let's repeat the experiment with waves. Imagine a tank of water with the same double-slit barrier. As you generate waves, they pass through both slits. On the other side, the two new sets of circular waves interfere with each other. Where the crest of one wave meets the crest of another, they combine to create a bigger wave. Where a crest meets a trough, they cancel each other out. The result on the detector screen is not two simple bands, but a characteristic "interference pattern" of many bands, with areas of high intensity alternating with areas of zero intensity. This pattern is the unmistakable signature of wave behavior.

Now for the quantum leap. Let's perform the experiment with electrons, the tiny particles that orbit the nucleus of an atom. We'll turn the intensity of our electron gun down so low that only one electron passes through the apparatus at a time. This ensures that the electrons aren't bumping into each other and interfering in some mundane way. Each electron flies towards the barrier, passes through, and makes a single, tiny dot on the detector screen. They are clearly arriving as individual particles, just like the paintballs.

If we let this process run for a while, collecting thousands of these individual dots, a stunning picture begins to emerge. The dots do not form two simple bands as the paintballs did. Instead, they form a perfect interference pattern, exactly as the water waves did. This is profoundly strange. It's as if each individual electron, traveling alone, somehow passed through *both* slits simultaneously, interfering with itself before landing on the screen. The electron behaves like a particle when it is detected (making a single dot), but it seems to behave like a wave as it travels through the experiment. This bizarre, seemingly contradictory nature is known as wave-particle duality.

This result is so counter-intuitive that physicists naturally wanted to peek behind the curtain. They decided to place a detector right by the slits to see which one each electron actually went through. With this detector in place, they fired the electrons one by one again. Sure enough, the detector registered each electron passing through either the left slit or the right slit, never both. But when they looked at the pattern that built up on the back screen, the interference pattern was gone. All they saw were two simple bands, just as if they had been firing paintballs.

This is the central mystery of quantum mechanics. The very act of observing which path the electron took forced it to "make a choice" and behave like a well-behaved particle. By measuring the system, the experimenters had fundamentally altered the outcome. It's not that the detector disturbed the electron's path in a classical sense, like a gust of wind. The mere acquisition of information— knowing which slit it went through—was enough to destroy the wave-like behavior. The quantum world, it seems, does not like to be watched. Before the measurement, the electron existed in a fuzzy, probabilistic state of possibilities. It was not in a single place, but was described by a "wave function," a mathematical expression that captured the probability of finding it at any given point. Passing through the slits, this wave function interfered with itself. The moment of measurement forced this cloud of possibilities to collapse into a single, definite reality.

This leads us to one of the most important concepts in quantum mechanics, and the first pillar of quantum computing: superposition. Before it was measured, the electron was in a superposition of states. It was in a blended state of "having gone through the left slit" AND "having gone through the right slit." It wasn't one or the other; it was, in a very real sense, both at the same time. This is not like a spinning coin which is simply an unknown state that will be revealed. In the quantum world, the state is genuinely indefinite until the moment of measurement.

This principle of superposition is not just a theoretical curiosity. It is the raw material from which quantum computation is built. A classical bit is fundamentally limited. It can be a 0 or a 1. It is a light switch that is either on or off. A quantum bit, or qubit, can also be a 0 or a 1. But thanks to the principle of superposition, it can also be in a combination of both states simultaneously. It is this ability to exist in a rich spectrum of possibilities at once that gives a quantum computer its extraordinary power. It can explore a vast number of potential solutions to a problem in a way that a classical computer, which must check each one sequentially, never could.

Another equally strange property of the quantum realm, which we will explore in detail later, is entanglement. It's possible to link two quantum particles in such a way that their fates become intertwined. No matter how far apart they are, a measurement on one particle instantly influences the state of the other. Einstein was so disturbed by this idea of instantaneous, faster-than-light correlation that he famously called it "spooky action at a distance." Yet, experiment after experiment has confirmed that this spooky connection is a real and fundamental feature of our universe. Entanglement provides a powerful resource for quantum computers, allowing for complex correlations and computational shortcuts that have no classical analogue.

So, what is the quantum realm? It is a world built on staircases, not ramps, where energy and other properties come in discrete packets. It is a world where particles are also waves, existing as clouds of probability until they are observed. It is a world governed by superposition, where an object can be in multiple states at once, and entanglement, where particles can be linked in spooky, instantaneous ways. It is a world that is fundamentally probabilistic, not deterministic. We can never know with certainty what a quantum system will do next; we can only calculate the odds.

This departure from the clockwork certainty of classical physics can be unsettling. It seems to fly in the face of our everyday experience. But that is only because we are large, warm, classical beings, built from an unimaginably vast number of quantum particles. The strange quantum effects average out over these huge collections of atoms, resulting in the solid, predictable world we know. But at the level of individual electrons, photons, and atoms—the level at which a quantum computer operates—this strange and wonderful logic is the only game in town. The challenge, and the opportunity, of quantum computing is to learn the rules of this game and harness them to build machines that can compute in a fundamentally new way.

CHAPTER THREE: Classical vs. Quantum: A Tale of Two Computers

Imagine you have two tools designed to create maps. The first is a state-of-the-art printer. It is incredibly precise, fast, and reliable. It can print any two-dimensional map you desire with stunning detail, laying down dots of ink in a perfectly ordered grid. It can render coastlines, cities, and roads with near-perfect accuracy. For navigating the flat surface of a piece of paper, this tool is unparalleled. This is your classical computer. It is a master of the flat, predictable, and deterministic world of bits.

The second tool is something altogether different. It is a holographic projector. Instead of printing a flat map, it generates a full, three-dimensional globe of light that floats in the middle of the room. You can walk around it, view it from any angle, and see the complex, curved relationships between continents in a way the flat map could never capture. However, the image is delicate. A stray breeze can make it flicker, and to get a specific piece of information, like the exact coordinates of a city, you have to "pin" the globe, at which point the entire shimmering projection collapses into that single, solid point of light. This is your quantum computer. It operates in a world of higher dimensions, probabilities, and delicate interconnections.

This analogy cuts to the heart of the matter: a quantum computer is not simply a more powerful version of a classical computer, just as a holographic globe is not simply a better printed map. They are fundamentally different kinds of devices, built on different physical principles, designed to process information in profoundly different ways, and suited for entirely different classes of problems. To truly appreciate the new frontier of quantum computing, we must first understand the deep-seated distinctions that separate it from the familiar digital world we inhabit every day. The story of their differences is a tale of two computers.

The most basic point of divergence lies in their fundamental unit of information. As we've seen, the classical computer is built upon the bit. The bit is the embodiment of certainty. It is a simple switch that can be in one of two definite states: 0 or 1, on or off, true or false. There is no ambiguity. This binary, black-and-white nature is the bedrock of all classical computation. Every piece of software, every website, and every digital photograph is, at its most granular level, an enormous collection of these definitive, unwavering ones and zeros. The strength of the classical bit is its reliability and simplicity.

The quantum computer, on the other hand, uses the qubit. A qubit can certainly be a 0 or a 1, just like a classical bit. If it were only this, it wouldn't be very interesting. The magic happens because a qubit can also exist in a superposition of both states at the same time. It is not a 0, nor is it a 1; it is a delicate, probabilistic blend of the two. Think back to our spinning coin. Before it lands, it is in a superposition of heads and tails. The qubit is in a similar state of potential, described by a wave function that captures the probability of it being a 0 and the probability of it being a 1 upon measurement.

To visualize this, imagine the classical bit as a light switch fixed in either the "up" (1) or "down" (0) position. The qubit is more like a dimmer switch. It can be fully up or fully down, but it can also be at any point in between, representing a weighted combination of the two states. An even better analogy is to picture a globe. The North Pole could represent the state 1, and the South Pole could represent the state 0. A classical bit can only ever be at one of these two poles. A qubit, however, can point to *any* location on the entire surface of the globe. This gives it access to a vastly richer and more complex informational space.

This fundamental difference in the nature of the bit versus the qubit leads to the most spectacular divergence between the two computing paradigms: how they scale. In a classical computer, the relationship between the number of bits and the amount of information they can store is straightforwardly linear. If you have 8 bits, you can store one of 2^8 (or 256) possible combinations, but you can only store *one* of them at a time. To represent the number 7, you set your bits to `00000111`. To represent the number 10, you set them to `00001010`. If you have N bits, you can represent 2^N possible values, but you must always choose just one.

Quantum computers blow this limitation out of the water. Thanks to superposition, a register of N qubits can, in a sense, represent all 2^N possible values *simultaneously*. Two qubits can exist in a superposition of the states 00, 01, 10, and 11. Three qubits can be in a superposition of all eight possible combinations (000, 001, 010, 011, 100, 101, 110, 111). With each additional qubit, the number of states it can simultaneously represent doubles. The information capacity grows exponentially.

This scaling is mind-bogglingly powerful. A classical computer with 300 bits can still only store one 300-character string of ones and zeros at a time. A quantum computer with 300 qubits, however, can exist in a superposition of 2^{300} states. This is a number so colossal that it is larger than the estimated number of atoms in the known universe. It is this exponential information density that forms the basis of a quantum computer's potential power. It can create and manipulate an informational space of unimaginable vastness, one that no classical computer could ever hope to even represent, let alone compute with.

This exponential scaling in information storage naturally leads to a completely different method of processing. A classical computer, for the most part, works sequentially. It takes an input, performs an operation, gets a result, and moves on to the next operation. Even with modern multi-core processors, which allow for a degree of parallel processing, the machine is essentially just performing a few separate sequential tasks at the same time. It's like a team of cooks, each following their own recipe step-by-step.

A quantum computer operates on a principle often called quantum parallelism. When you perform an operation—a quantum gate—on a register of qubits that are in a superposition of states, you are performing that operation on *all* of those states at the very same time. It's not that the computer is secretly running millions of calculations in parallel; it is performing a single, complex operation on one fantastically rich quantum state.

Let's return to the maze analogy. A classical computer trying to find the exit would be like a person walking down every single possible path, one after the other, until they find the right one. For a complex maze, this could take an eternity. A quantum computer is more like flooding the entire maze with water at once. The water flows down every path simultaneously, and the first place it emerges reveals the shortest path to the exit. This ability to explore a problem's entire landscape of solutions in a single computational step is what allows quantum algorithms to solve certain problems exponentially faster than their classical counterparts.

This brings us to another critical, and deeply counter-intuitive, difference: the act of getting an answer. In a classical computer, reading the state of a bit is a simple and non-destructive act. If a bit is a 1, you can look at it a million times, and it will still be a 1. The information is solid, stable, and easily accessible. The process of observation does not change the data being observed.

In the quantum world, observation is a dramatic and world-altering event. As we saw in the double-slit experiment, the moment you measure a quantum system, its rich state of superposition collapses into a single, definite classical outcome. If you measure a qubit that is in a superposition of 0 and 1, it will be forced to "choose" one of those states. The wave function collapses, and the vast quantum information it held—the probabilities, the relationships between states—is largely lost, leaving you with just a single classical bit of information.

This has profound consequences for how you get an answer from a quantum computer. You can't just "read out" the rich superpositional state in the middle of a calculation. The act of reading it would destroy it. Instead, a quantum algorithm is carefully designed to manipulate the probabilities of all the possible states. The goal is to choreograph the quantum waves of possibility so that they interfere with each other, canceling out the waves corresponding to wrong answers and amplifying the waves corresponding to the right answer.

At the end of the computation, you perform a measurement. Because of the carefully designed interference, the probability of the state collapsing to the correct answer is now very high. However, it is never one hundred percent certain. A quantum computer is a probabilistic machine, not a deterministic one. This means that for most quantum algorithms, you have to run the entire computation multiple times and look at the statistical distribution of the results. The answer that appears most frequently is, with very high probability, the correct one. A classical computer gives you a single, definite answer. A quantum computer gives you a set of highly probable answers.

This inherent fragility of quantum states points to yet another major practical difference: their relationship with the environment. Classical bits are incredibly robust. It takes a significant physical event, like a jolt of static electricity or a cosmic ray, to flip a bit in your laptop's memory. Modern electronics are designed to be stable and resilient against the minor fluctuations of the everyday world. We have perfected the art of classical error correction over decades, making our machines extraordinarily reliable.

Qubits, by contrast, are the snowflakes of the computing world. They are exquisitely sensitive to their surroundings. The very quantum properties that make them so powerful—superposition and entanglement—are incredibly delicate. The slightest interaction with the outside world, a stray vibration, a tiny change in temperature, or a weak electromagnetic field, can be enough to disturb the quantum state and cause its superposition to collapse. This process is called decoherence. It is the arch-nemesis of quantum computing, the constant "noise" that threatens to wash away the quantum information before a computation can be completed.

Building a quantum computer is therefore less like building a new type of microchip and more like building the world's most sensitive scientific instrument inside the world's quietest room.

They require extreme isolation, often being cooled to temperatures colder than deep space, shielded from magnetic fields, and suspended in vacuums to protect their fragile qubits from the disruptive influence of the classical world. Taming this noise and developing quantum error correction is one of the single greatest engineering challenges of our time.

Finally, these profound differences in operation mean that classical and quantum computers are suited for completely different tasks. A quantum computer will not be replacing your laptop for writing emails or your smartphone for browsing social media. For these everyday tasks, classical computers are, and will likely remain, far superior. They are fast, cheap, reliable, and perfectly suited for the deterministic, logical problems that dominate our digital lives. Using a quantum computer to add two numbers together would be like using a space shuttle to go to the grocery store—a spectacular and inefficient waste of a specialized tool.

Quantum computers are specialized machines designed for a specific set of problems that are intractable for classical computers. These are problems where the immense, exponential complexity of a quantum system is a feature, not a bug. They excel at simulating other quantum systems, a task Richard Feynman envisioned decades ago. This could revolutionize drug discovery and materials science by allowing us to model molecular interactions with perfect fidelity. They are also uniquely suited for certain types of optimization problems, like finding the most efficient routes for a global logistics network, and, most famously, for breaking modern cryptographic codes by factoring large numbers, a task that relies on the quantum ability to find periodic patterns.

So, we are left with a tale of two very different protagonists. The classical computer is the reliable workhorse, the master of logic and order, built on the certainty of the bit. It processes information sequentially in a flat, binary landscape. The quantum computer is the exotic explorer, the master of probability and complexity, built on the potential of the qubit. It navigates a vast, high-dimensional space, exploring all possibilities at once. One is a tool of deterministic precision; the other, a tool of probabilistic power. They are not competitors, but complements. The future of computing will not be a story of one replacing the other, but of these two different machines working in concert, each tackling the problems for which it is uniquely designed.

CHAPTER FOUR: The Qubit: Building Block of the Quantum World

In the world of classical computing, we have a hero. It is a humble, dependable, and incredibly straightforward character: the bit. This fundamental unit of information is the bedrock of our digital civilization, a simple switch that operates on a principle of absolute certainty. It is either a 0 or a 1, on or off, black or white. There is no middle ground, no ambiguity. Its strength lies in this unwavering simplicity. From this binary foundation, we have constructed castles of logic and silicon that have reshaped the world. Yet, as we stand at the precipice of a new computational era, we find that this hero, for all its accomplishments, has its limits. To venture further, we need a new protagonist, one born from the strange and probabilistic laws of the quantum realm. It's time to meet the qubit.

The qubit, short for "quantum bit," is the fundamental unit of information in a quantum computer. On the surface, it shares a family resemblance with its classical cousin. A qubit can, after all, represent a 0 or a 1. If you measure a qubit, it will always give you a definite answer, either 0 or 1, just like a classical bit. This is a crucial point; the output of a quantum computation, at the end of the day, must be a string of classical bits that we can read and understand. However, the story of what the qubit is doing *before* that final measurement is where the revolution truly lies. Where the classical bit is a simple light switch, the qubit is a shimmering, multi-dimensional entity of pure potential.

To get a proper handle on the identity of a qubit, we need a better way to visualize it than a simple on-off switch. The most widely used and intuitive model is a conceptual tool known as the Bloch Sphere. Imagine a perfect globe. The South Pole of this globe represents the definite classical state of 0, and the North Pole represents the definite classical state of 1. A classical bit can only ever be at one of these two poles. It's either fully south or fully north. There are no other options. The state of a qubit, however, can be represented by an arrow, or a vector, originating from the center of the sphere and pointing to *any* spot on its surface.

This opens up a whole new world of possibilities. If the arrow points directly down to the South Pole, the qubit is in the state 0. If it points directly up to the North Pole, it's in the state 1. But what if it points to the equator? A point on the equator is equidistant from both poles. In this case, the qubit is in a perfect, 50/50 superposition of both 0 and 1. If you were to measure a qubit in this state, you would have an exactly equal chance of getting a 0 or a 1. It's the quantum equivalent of a perfectly balanced, spinning coin just before it lands.

But the qubit is not limited to the poles and the equator. The arrow can point anywhere on the surface of the sphere. If it points to a location in the northern hemisphere, for instance, it is still in a superposition of 0 and 1, but it is now "biased" towards the 1 state. The closer the arrow points to the North Pole, the higher the probability that a measurement will yield a 1. Conversely, an arrow pointing to the southern hemisphere represents a superposition biased towards the 0 state. The latitude of our arrow's destination on the sphere, its angle relative to the vertical axis, tells us the probability of measuring a 0 or a 1. This gives the qubit an infinite number of possible superpositional states, a continuous spectrum of possibilities that the classical bit, stuck at its two poles, can only dream of.

To discuss these states more precisely, physicists use a standard notation known as Dirac notation, or "ket" notation. It looks a little intimidating at first, but it is essentially just a fancy form of labeling. The classical state 0 is written as $|0\rangle$, and the classical state 1 is written as $|1\rangle$. These two states, corresponding to the South and North poles of our Bloch Sphere, are known as the "basis states." They form the fundamental reference points from which all other qubit states are described. Think of them as the primary colors of the quantum palette.

Using this notation, we can write the general state of any qubit as a combination, or superposition, of these two basis states. The formal way to write this is:

$$|\psi\rangle = \alpha|0\rangle + \beta|1\rangle$$

Here, $|\psi\rangle$ (pronounced "psi") represents the state of our qubit—the direction of the arrow on our Bloch Sphere. The symbols α (alpha) and β (beta) are the crucial new ingredients. They are not simple numbers; they are special types of numbers called "probability amplitudes." These amplitudes tell us everything we need to know about the qubit's state. They are complex numbers, meaning they have both a magnitude and a direction (or phase), but for now, let's focus on their magnitude. The magnitude of these amplitudes determines the probability of our measurement outcome.

The rule is simple: the probability of measuring the qubit and finding it in the state $|0\rangle$ is equal to the magnitude of alpha squared, written as $|\alpha|^2$. The probability of finding it in the state $|1\rangle$ is the magnitude of beta squared, $|\beta|^2$. This is the mathematical engine behind our Bloch Sphere analogy. The latitude of our arrow is directly determined by the values of $|\alpha|^2$ and $|\beta|^2$. If our qubit is in the state $|0\rangle$, then α is 1 and β is 0. The probability of measuring 0 is $|1|^2$, which is 1 (or 100%), and the probability of measuring 1 is $|0|^2$, which is 0. This makes perfect sense.

Because these are the only two possible outcomes of a measurement, the sum of their probabilities must always equal 1. This gives us the fundamental rule for any qubit state: $|\alpha|^2 + |\beta|^2 = 1$. This is a mathematical way of saying that the arrow must always touch the surface of the Bloch Sphere, never fall short or extend beyond it. It ensures that our probabilities always add up to 100%. If a qubit is in an equal superposition, as represented by a point on the equator of the sphere, the probability of getting 0 is 0.5 and the probability of getting 1 is 0.5. This corresponds to alpha and beta having equal magnitudes.

So far, we have only talked about the magnitude of the amplitudes, which corresponds to the latitude on our Bloch Sphere. But this is only half the story. The amplitudes α and β also have a property called "phase." In our globe analogy, if latitude tells you how far north or south you are, phase tells you your longitude—your rotational position around the sphere's axis. This introduces a second, hidden layer of information to the qubit's state that has no classical counterpart. Two qubits can have the exact same probability of collapsing to 0 or 1, but still be in fundamentally different quantum states if their relative phase is different. They might both be on the same line of latitude on the Bloch Sphere, but at different longitudes.

For a single, isolated qubit, this phase information is invisible. If you measure a qubit, the outcome depends only on the magnitudes of α and β. The phase information seems to play no role. It's like being on the equator; your chances of seeing a polar bear or a penguin don't change whether you're in Ecuador or Kenya. So, why is phase so important? The answer is that phase becomes the most critical factor of all when qubits start to interact with each other and with quantum operations. Phase is the secret ingredient that makes quantum interference possible.

Interference is the heart of what makes a quantum algorithm powerful. As we saw in the double-slit experiment, waves can interfere constructively (building each other up) or destructively (canceling each other out). The probability amplitudes of a qubit behave like waves. The phase of the amplitude is what determines how these waves will line up. By carefully manipulating the phases of qubits, a quantum algorithm can choreograph a dance of interference on a massive scale. It can arrange things so that the amplitudes corresponding to incorrect answers destructively interfere, their probabilities dwindling to zero, while the amplitudes corresponding to the correct answer constructively interfere, amplifying its probability to be near one.

Think of it like listening to music with two speakers. If the sound waves from both speakers arrive at your ear perfectly aligned (in phase), the sound is loud and clear. If they arrive perfectly misaligned, with the peak of one wave meeting the trough of the other (out of phase), they can cancel each other out, resulting in silence. The volume you hear depends on both the amplitude (the loudness from each speaker) and the relative phase (how the waves are aligned). In a quantum computer, the "music" is the computation, and quantum gates are the tools we use to precisely adjust both the amplitude and the phase of our qubits to ensure the right answer is the one we hear at the end.

This brings us to a common and tantalizing misconception about the qubit. Since a qubit's state can be represented by a point on a continuous sphere, described by two numbers (α and β) that can take on an infinite range of values, does this mean a single qubit can store an infinite amount of information? It's a beautiful idea, but unfortunately, it's not true. This is perhaps the most counter-intuitive aspect of the qubit: despite its seemingly infinite capacity to *hold* information in a delicate superpositional state, you can only ever *extract* one single classical bit of information from it.

The moment you perform a measurement on the qubit, the magic is over. The shimmering globe of possibilities collapses into one of its two classical poles. The arrow is forced to snap to either the North Pole ($|1\rangle$) or the South Pole ($|0\rangle$). All of the nuanced information about the specific superposition it was in—the exact values of its amplitudes and its phase—is instantly and irretrievably lost. You are left with a simple 0 or 1. The vast, high-dimensional quantum information collapses into a single bit of classical information. This limitation, formalized in a result known as Holevo's theorem, is a fundamental feature of our universe.

So, if you can only get one bit of information out of a qubit, what's the point? The power of the qubit is not in being a super-dense storage device. Its power is revealed during computation, *before* the measurement. The true strength of quantum computing comes from stringing many qubits together. When you have a system of multiple qubits, they can become entangled, their fates intertwined in a complex, high-dimensional space that grows exponentially with each added qubit. The computation involves manipulating this entire complex state, leveraging both superposition and phase to guide the system towards a desired outcome. The final measurement is just the last step, where we peek into this vast computational space to retrieve the highly probable answer that the algorithm has prepared for us.

It's also important to remember that a qubit is not just a mathematical abstraction. It is a real, physical object. While the Bloch Sphere and the $\alpha|0\rangle + \beta|1\rangle$ equation provide a universal language for describing a qubit, the hardware that embodies it can take many forms. A qubit could be an individual electron, where its intrinsic property of "spin" can be either "up" ($|1\rangle$) or "down" ($|0\rangle$). It could be a single photon, where its polarization can be either horizontal ($|1\rangle$) or vertical ($|0\rangle$). It could also be a tiny, superconducting circuit, where two different, discrete energy levels in an artificial atom correspond to the $|0\rangle$ and $|1\rangle$ states. Each of these physical systems, and many others, can be controlled and manipulated to behave according to the rules of the qubit.

The specific engineering challenges of building and controlling these physical qubits are immense, and they will be the subject of a later chapter. The key takeaway for now is that the abstract concept of the qubit is a unifying principle. Just as the idea of a "bit" can be represented by a hole in a punch card, a magnetic domain on a hard drive, or a voltage level in a silicon transistor, the "qubit" is a platform-agnostic concept. It is the fundamental atom of quantum information, the building block upon which the entire edifice of quantum computation is constructed. It is a system that can be 0, 1, or a probabilistic blend of both, infused with a hidden phase that unlocks the power of quantum interference. Understanding this strange and powerful object is the first true step into the larger world of quantum computation.

CHAPTER FIVE: Superposition: The Power of Being in Two Places at Once

Of all the strange concepts that sprout from the soil of quantum mechanics, superposition is perhaps the most foundational and the most frequently misunderstood. It is the principle that underpins the qubit's power and grants a quantum computer its almost mythical computational prowess. We have encountered it briefly in the baffling behavior of an electron in the double-slit experiment, which seemed to pass through both slits at once, and we've seen it represented as an arrow pointing anywhere on the surface of the Bloch Sphere. But to truly grasp the quantum revolution, we must move beyond these initial glimpses and confront the idea head-on. What does it really mean for something to be in two states at the same time?

A common but slightly misleading analogy is that of a spinning coin. While it's in the air, it is neither heads nor tails. This captures the idea of an undecided state, but it misses a crucial quantum subtlety. The spinning coin has a definite, albeit unknown, state at all times; if we had a super-camera, we could freeze a frame and see which side was up. A qubit in superposition is fundamentally different. It is not in an unknown state, but in a genuinely indefinite one. There is no hidden information to uncover. Its reality is smeared out across its possibilities until a measurement forces it to take a stand.

A more fitting analogy might be found in the world of music. Imagine a single key pressed on a piano. This is a classical bit, a definite note, a C or a G. It is one thing and one thing only. A superposition is like playing a musical chord. When you press three keys at once to play a C-major chord, you are not hearing a C, then an E, then a G. You are not hearing an "unknown" note that will resolve itself into one of the three. You are hearing a single, richer, more complex entity: the chord itself. It is a new state that is a combination of its constituent notes, existing as one coherent whole. A qubit in superposition is a similar kind of computational chord, a single entity that holds the information of both 0 and 1 within its state.

This "both-at-once-ness" is the first pillar of quantum power. Let's return to the mathematical language of the qubit we introduced in the previous chapter: $|\psi\rangle = \alpha|0\rangle + \beta|1\rangle$. This equation is the recipe for our quantum chord. The basis states, $|0\rangle$ and $|1\rangle$, are the individual notes, while the probability amplitudes, α and β, tell us how much of each note to include in the mix. An operation on a classical bit is like changing a single note to another. An operation in a quantum computer, however, is like a musical transformation that affects the entire chord at once, altering the balance between all the notes in a single, fluid step.

We can visualize this on the Bloch Sphere. Preparing a qubit in the $|0\rangle$ state is equivalent to placing its state vector at the South Pole. Now, imagine we want to put it into a superposition. The quantum equivalent of this action is to apply an operation that rotates the vector off the pole. For instance, we could apply a precise pulse of energy that rotates the vector 90 degrees, moving it from the South Pole right up to the equator. Now, our qubit is no longer in a definite state. It is in a perfect 50/50 superposition of $|0\rangle$ and $|1\rangle$. It is at a point on its globe of possibilities that is exactly halfway between the two classical extremes.

This ability to manipulate a qubit's state—to rotate its vector around the Bloch Sphere—is the fundamental act of quantum computation. By applying a sequence of these controlled rotations, we can guide the qubit's state to any point on the sphere, adjusting the amplitudes α and β with incredible precision. This gives us fine-tuned control over the probability of the final outcome. We can create a state that is 70% likely to be a 1 and 30% likely to be a 0, or 99% likely to be a 0 and 1% likely to be a 1. This level of analog control over a digital system is completely foreign to classical computing.

While manipulating a single qubit in this way is interesting, the true explosion of computational power occurs when we bring multiple qubits together. This is where the exponential nature of quantum mechanics truly begins to shine. If we have two classical bits, we can represent one of four possible states at any given time: 00, 01, 10, or 11. That's it. To work with a different state, you have to erase the old one and write the new one. A two-qubit system, however, can exist in a superposition of all four of these states simultaneously.

Let's extend our musical analogy. A two-qubit system isn't just a single chord; it's more like a harmony played by two different instruments. It can be in a complex state that is a blend of all four possible combinations of their individual notes. Its state is described by a more complex equation with four parts: $|\psi\rangle = \alpha|00\rangle + \beta|01\rangle + \gamma|10\rangle + \delta|11\rangle$. Each of the amplitudes (α, β, γ, δ) governs the probability of finding the system in that particular classical state upon measurement. And just as before, the sum of the squared magnitudes of these amplitudes must equal one.

Now, let's scale this up. For three qubits, we can exist in a superposition of eight states (from $|000\rangle$ to $|111\rangle$). For four qubits, it's sixteen states. For N qubits, the system can exist in a single, complex quantum state that is a superposition of all 2^N possible classical states. This is the source of the almost unbelievable information capacity of a quantum computer. A mere 300 qubits can hold more classical states in superposition than there are atoms in the known universe. This is a computational arena so vast it is literally astronomical in scale.

This property leads to a powerful concept known as quantum parallelism. Suppose you have a function, let's call it $f(x)$, and you want to evaluate this function for many different input values of x. A classical computer must do this sequentially. It calculates $f(0)$, then $f(1)$, then $f(2)$, and so on. It is a one-by-one process. A quantum computer can take a completely different approach. It can prepare a register of qubits in a superposition of all possible input values. For an N-qubit register, this means preparing a state that is an equal mix of every number from 0 to $2^N - 1$.

Then, by applying a sequence of quantum operations that corresponds to the function `f`, the computer can evaluate the function for every single one of those values in a single computational step. The single quantum operation acts on the entire superposition at once, transforming the state into a new superposition that contains the results of all the calculations. It's as if you could whisper a question to the universe and receive, in an instant, a shimmering cloud containing every possible answer. You have, in one fell swoop, calculated `f(x)` for millions or billions of values simultaneously.

This sounds like magic. It seems we have found the ultimate computational shortcut, a way to perform an exponential number of calculations in a single go. However, there is a catch, and it is a very big one. This spectacular parallel computation happens within the private, sealed-off quantum realm. The result is a complex superposition containing all the answers. But remember what happens when we try to look at a quantum state: measurement. The moment we measure our output register, the delicate superposition shatters, and we are left with just one single, randomly chosen result from the vast sea of possibilities.

If you calculate a million values in superposition and then measure, you will get just one of those million values back. Which one? The laws of quantum mechanics say that the outcome is probabilistic. In the simplest case, where all answers are equally likely, it's like getting one random answer from a hat containing a million slips of paper. You have performed a million calculations just to get one random result. This is no better—and in fact, is far more difficult and expensive—than just running the calculation once on a classical computer. This is the great challenge and the central paradox of quantum algorithm design. We have access to this immense parallel workspace, but we are only allowed to peek at the final result through a tiny, probabilistic pinhole.

So, how do we make superposition useful? How do we extract a meaningful signal from this computational noise? The answer lies in the second great principle of quantum mechanics: interference. A quantum algorithm is not simply about computing in superposition. It is a carefully choreographed dance designed to manipulate the probability amplitudes of the quantum state. The goal is to make the amplitudes of all the wrong answers destructively interfere—to cancel each other out like waves meeting trough-to-trough—while making the amplitudes of the correct answer constructively interfere, amplifying its probability of being the one we see upon measurement.

A quantum algorithm is a recipe for focusing this vast, parallel quantum state down to a single, highly probable, and correct answer. It's like a searchlight in a dark room full of possibilities. Instead of lighting up the whole room dimly (a uniform superposition), the algorithm swivels and focuses the beam until one spot, the right answer, is brilliantly illuminated, while the rest of the room is plunged into darkness. The final measurement is then almost certain to reveal the location of that bright spot.

To see how this works in practice, let's consider one of the simplest and earliest examples that demonstrated a true quantum advantage. It's a toy problem, but a brilliant one, known as Deutsch's Problem, formulated by physicist David Deutsch in 1985. Imagine you are given a "black box" that computes a function on a single bit. The input can be 0 or 1, and the output can be 0 or 1. You are promised that the function inside the box is one of two types: it is either *constant* (it gives the same output for both inputs, so $f(0) = f(1)$) or it is *balanced* (it gives a different output for each input, so $f(0) \neq f(1)$). Your job is to figure out which type of function is in the box.

Using a classical computer, the solution is straightforward but requires two steps. You must first query the box with the input 0 to find $f(0)$. Then you must query it a second time with the input 1 to find $f(1)$. Only after you have both results can you compare them and determine if the function is constant or balanced. There is no way around it. You have to check both inputs. Two queries are the absolute minimum required to solve the problem.

A quantum computer, however, can do better. It can solve the problem in a single query. The process begins by preparing an input qubit not as a definite 0 or 1, but in a superposition of both. This "ask about both inputs at once" state is then fed into a quantum version of the black box. The magic happens inside the box. As the quantum state passes through, the function is evaluated for both the $|0\rangle$ and $|1\rangle$ components simultaneously. But it doesn't just produce an output; it uses the properties of the function to impart a subtle change to the quantum state, specifically to its phase.

If the function is constant, the two parts of the superposition are affected in one way. If the function is balanced, they are affected in a different way. The nature of the function—its "global" property of being constant or balanced—is imprinted onto the phase relationship of the output superposition. The quantum computer doesn't need to know the individual values of $f(0)$ and $f(1)$. It only needs to know how they relate to each other, and this relationship is encoded directly into the wave-like properties of the resulting quantum state.

After this single pass through the function, a final set of operations is performed on the output qubit. This step is designed to act as an interference filter. It transforms the phase information, which is normally hidden from measurement, into amplitude information that we can see. If the function was constant, the state is manipulated in such a way that it is guaranteed to collapse to 0 upon measurement. If the function was balanced, the very same manipulation guarantees that it will collapse to 1. By making one single measurement, we can determine the nature of the function with 100% certainty. One quantum query achieves what takes a classical computer two.

This might seem like a modest gain, but it is a monumental proof of principle. It shows that by leveraging superposition and interference, a quantum computer can solve a problem more efficiently than any possible classical computer. It accesses a type of information—a global property of a function—in a way that is simply unavailable to a machine that must check each input one by one. The algorithm "feels out" the entire function at once and returns a single bit that describes its overall character.

This principle is the blueprint for more complex and world-changing quantum algorithms. The ability to prepare a system in a superposition of a vast number of states, to process all of them simultaneously with a quantum operation, and then to use interference to distill that massive computation down to a single, useful answer is the fundamental pattern of quantum computation. Superposition is not just a strange physical quirk; it is the key that unlocks a computational workspace exponentially larger than our own, providing the raw material and the parallel power that fuels the quantum age.

CHAPTER SIX: Entanglement: Einstein's "Spooky Action at a Distance"

If superposition is the strange solo act of the quantum world, allowing a single particle to take on multiple identities at once, then entanglement is its breathtaking and deeply mysterious ensemble performance. It is a phenomenon so bizarre, so contrary to our ingrained sense of how the universe ought to work, that it famously prompted Albert Einstein to give it a name that has stuck ever since: *spukhafte Fernwirkung*, or "spooky action at a distance." It is the second, and arguably more profound, pillar of quantum computing, a resource that binds the fates of quantum particles together in a way that transcends the normal rules of space and time.

To begin to understand entanglement, let's first consider a perfectly normal, non-spooky situation. Imagine we have a pair of gloves, one right-handed and one left-handed. We place them into two identical, sealed boxes without looking. We keep one box and give the other to a friend who boards a spaceship and travels to the Andromeda galaxy, two and a half million light-years away. You wait for a few million years, and then, on a designated Tuesday, you open your box. Inside, you find the right-handed glove. At that exact instant, with a certainty that is absolute, you know something about the box in the Andromeda galaxy: it contains the left-handed glove.

There is nothing particularly mysterious about this. The information about the other glove didn't travel faster than light from your box to your friend's. The outcome was pre-determined from the very beginning, the moment the gloves were placed in the boxes. The properties of the gloves—their "handedness"—were definite and distinct all along. Your act of opening the box simply revealed a piece of information that was already there. This is what physicists call a classical correlation. It's a perfectly sensible, local, and realistic view of the world. This, in essence, is what Einstein and his colleagues, Boris Podolsky and Nathan Rosen, believed must be happening at the quantum level as well. Quantum mechanics, they argued in a landmark 1935 paper, must be incomplete. There must be "hidden variables," like the pre-determined handedness of the gloves, that dictate the outcome of measurements.

The universe, however, had other ideas. Quantum entanglement is not like the pair of gloves. It is far, far stranger. Imagine we create two quantum particles, say two qubits, in a special, entangled state. We can arrange it so that they have opposite properties. For instance, we can entangle their spin, a quantum property that can be measured as either "up" or "down." We create the pair in a state such that we know for certain their spins will be opposite: if one is measured as up, the other must be down, and vice-versa. Now, just like with the gloves, we put these two qubits in separate boxes and send one to the Andromeda galaxy.

Here is the crucial, mind-bending difference. According to the laws of quantum mechanics, before you make a measurement, neither qubit has a definite spin. It's not that you just don't know what the spin is; the property of spin itself is undefined for each individual particle. Each qubit is in a perfect superposition of both up and down. They are like two ghostly, spinning coins, with their individual outcomes entirely undecided. The only thing that is definite is the relationship between them—the fact that they will be opposite. The system as a whole has a defined property, but its individual parts do not.

Now, you open your box and measure your qubit. The moment you do, its wave function collapses, and it randomly settles into a definite state, say, "spin up." At that very same instant, two and a half million light-years away, its entangled partner, which until that moment was also in a state of pure potential, immediately snaps into the state of "spin down." It's as if your measurement here on Earth forced the distant particle to make a choice. The correlation is instantaneous, appearing to defy the cosmic speed limit set by the speed of light. This is the "spooky action" that so troubled Einstein. It suggests a deep, holistic connection between the two particles, a bond that is indifferent to the distance separating them.

This concept can be represented using the ket notation we introduced for qubits. A simple entangled state for two qubits, known as a Bell state, can be written as:

$$|\psi\rangle = (1/\sqrt{2})(|01\rangle + |10\rangle)$$

Let's break this down. This equation describes the state of the *entire two-qubit system*. It tells us that the system is in an equal superposition of two possibilities: the first qubit is 0 and the second is 1 (the $|01\rangle$ part), OR the first qubit is 1 and the second is 0 (the $|10\rangle$ part). Notice that there are no terms for $|00\rangle$ or $|11\rangle$. Those outcomes are impossible in this state. If you measure the first qubit and find it to be a 0, the entire state instantly collapses to the only term consistent with that measurement: $|01\rangle$. The second qubit *must* be a 1. The two particles are no longer independent entities; their fates are described by a single, shared wave function. You cannot write down a description for the first qubit without simultaneously describing the second. They have lost their individual identities and have merged into a single, inseparable quantum state.

For decades, the debate raged. Was the universe like Einstein's gloves, with pre-determined properties we just couldn't see? Or was it as strange as quantum mechanics suggested, with genuinely undecided states and spooky non-local connections? The argument seemed almost philosophical, a matter of interpretation rather than testable science. That all changed in the 1960s thanks to the brilliant work of an Irish physicist named John Stewart Bell. He took the EPR paradox out of the realm of thought experiments and placed it firmly in the world of real, physical tests.

Bell devised a theorem, now known as Bell's theorem, that provided a mathematical way to distinguish between the two competing worldviews. He reasoned that if there were local "hidden variables"—if the particles were like the gloves, carrying secret instructions on how to behave when measured—then there would be a statistical limit to how strongly their properties could be correlated when measured at different angles. A classical universe governed by local reality has to play by certain statistical rules. Bell then showed that the predictions of quantum mechanics, for certain measurement setups, would violate this limit. The correlations predicted by quantum theory were stronger than any classical theory could ever allow.

Bell had thrown down a gauntlet. He had turned a philosophical debate into a concrete, experimental question: measure the correlations between entangled particles and see if they exceed the "Bell limit." If they do, then Einstein's comfortable, classical view of the universe is wrong, and the spooky, non-local reality of quantum mechanics is correct.

Beginning in the 1970s and continuing with increasing precision ever since, physicists have performed these experiments. One of the most famous and definitive early tests was conducted by a team led by French physicist Alain Aspect in 1982. These experiments typically involve creating pairs of entangled photons and sending them in opposite directions to detectors that can measure their polarization. The results have been unambiguous and have been replicated countless times. In experiment after experiment, Bell's inequality has been violated, and the statistical predictions of quantum mechanics have been confirmed with astonishing accuracy. The verdict of nature is in: spooky action is real. The universe is, at its heart, non-local.

This profound discovery naturally leads to a tantalizing question: can we use entanglement to communicate faster than the speed of light? If measuring a qubit here instantly affects a qubit on Andromeda, could we use that to send a message? Imagine you and your friend on Andromeda agree on a code: if you want to send a "1," you'll measure your qubit in a way that forces it into the "up" state. Your friend, seeing their qubit instantly snap to "down," would receive your "1." It seems like the perfect instantaneous communication device.

Unfortunately, the universe is more subtle than that. The answer is a definitive no. Entanglement cannot be used to transmit information faster than light. The reason lies in the inherent randomness of quantum measurement. When you measure your qubit, you cannot control the outcome. You have a 50% chance of getting "up" and a 50% chance of getting "down." While you instantly know what your friend's result will be, you have no way of dictating what that result is. You can't force your qubit to be "up" to send your message. You can only measure it and discover what it randomly decided to be.

Your friend on Andromeda also sees a completely random stream of results: up, down, down, up, up, down... It looks like pure static. Your results on Earth are also a random stream, but a perfectly anti-correlated one. The only way for your friend to know that their static is correlated with your static is for you to send them your list of results using a classical communication channel, like a radio signal. They can then compare the two lists and be amazed at the perfect correlation. But this classical signal, of course, can travel no faster than the speed of light. Entanglement creates a spooky correlation, but it does not provide a spooky communication channel.

So, if it can't be used for faster-than-light communication, why is entanglement so central to quantum computing? Because it is the ultimate computational resource. It is the thread that weaves individual qubits, each with their own superpositions, into a single, exponentially vast computational fabric. A quantum computer with N qubits is not just N separate systems. If they are entangled, they become one single system whose state is described in a massive mathematical space—a space with 2^N dimensions. It is this shared, holistic nature that allows a quantum computer to perform tasks that are impossible for classical machines.

Entanglement allows for a form of correlation and information processing that goes far beyond what superposition alone can offer. Consider what happens when you apply a quantum gate—an operation—to one qubit in an entangled pair. Because of their deep connection, this operation can affect the entire state of the system, influencing the potential outcomes of its distant partner in complex ways. This allows for intricate, parallel computations where the qubits work in a coordinated concert that is impossible to simulate classically.

This powerful resource is the key ingredient behind some of the most spectacular applications of quantum information science. In quantum cryptography, entangled particles can be used to create provably secure communication channels, where any attempt by an eavesdropper to intercept the message would instantly break the entanglement and reveal their presence. It is also the basis for "superdense coding," a protocol that allows you to transmit two classical bits of information by sending only a single qubit, provided the sender and receiver already share an entangled pair.

Perhaps the most famous application is quantum teleportation. This is not the "beam me up, Scotty" of science fiction, as it does not transport matter. Instead, it is a protocol for transmitting the exact, unknown quantum state of one qubit to another, distant qubit. This is achieved by using a pair of entangled qubits as a sort of quantum channel. The process involves making a joint measurement on the original qubit and one half of the entangled pair, and then sending the classical results of that measurement to the location of the other half of the pair. Based on those two classical bits of information, a final operation can be performed on the distant qubit to perfectly reconstruct the original state. The quantum state itself is destroyed in one location and recreated in another, without ever physically traversing the space between them.

In the context of computation, entanglement is the engine that drives the exponential scaling of quantum systems. When you have a register of 300 qubits, their power does not come from the fact that you have 300 independent spinning coins. Their power comes from the possibility of creating a single, vast, entangled state among all 300 of them. This single state explores a problem space with more possibilities than there are atoms in the universe. Quantum algorithms are designed to create and manipulate these highly entangled states, choreographing a complex, multi-particle interference pattern that guides the entire system towards the correct answer.

If superposition opens the door to quantum parallelism, allowing a computer to consider many inputs at once, entanglement provides the hallways and corridors that connect all the rooms. It ensures that the computation is a coherent, global process, not just a collection of independent calculations. Mastering the creation, control, and preservation of this delicate, spooky connection is one of the greatest experimental challenges in building a functional quantum computer, but it is also the source of its most profound and revolutionary potential.

CHAPTER SEVEN: Quantum Gates: The Language of Quantum Computers

If the qubits we have met are the letters of a new quantum alphabet, then we are still missing a crucial component before we can write anything meaningful. We need verbs. We need a set of actions, operations, and transformations that allow us to manipulate these letters, arrange them into words, and construct the powerful sentences of a quantum algorithm. In the world of computation, both classical and quantum, these verbs are called "gates." They are the fundamental building blocks of logic, the tiny, primitive operations that, when strung together in the right sequence, can perform everything from simple arithmetic to simulating the very fabric of the universe.

In the familiar realm of classical computing, we have a small but powerful toolkit of logic gates that have served as the foundation of the digital revolution for over half a century. You may have heard their names: AND, OR, NOT, XOR. The NOT gate is the simplest, a basic inverter that flips a 0 to a 1 and a 1 to a 0. The AND gate takes two bits as input and outputs a 1 only if *both* inputs are 1. The OR gate outputs a 1 if *either* of its inputs is a 1. From these simple, deterministic rules, engineers can construct circuits of staggering complexity that execute the software running on your phone or laptop. These gates are the atomic units of classical logic.

To build a quantum computer, we need a corresponding set of quantum gates. These gates will form the language that allows us to write quantum programs. They will be the tools we use to initialize our qubits, to coax them into states of superposition, to weave them together through entanglement, and to choreograph the delicate dance of interference that guides the computation to a useful answer. While they serve a similar purpose to their classical cousins, quantum gates operate according to a completely different and, in some ways, much stricter set of rules, dictated by the fundamental laws of quantum mechanics.

The first and most important of these new rules is the principle of reversibility. A quantum gate must always be reversible. This means that if you know the output of a gate, you must be able to work backward and figure out, with absolute certainty, what its input was. The operation must be a two-way street. Think of it like a rotation. If you take a statue and rotate it 90 degrees clockwise, you can always undo that operation by rotating it 90 degrees counter-clockwise to get back to the original state. The information about its initial orientation is never lost.

This stands in stark contrast to many classical gates. Consider the AND gate. If an AND gate outputs a 0, what were its two inputs? They could have been 0 and 0, or 0 and 1, or 1 and 0. There is no way to know for sure. Information has been lost in the process; two bits of input information were compressed into a single bit of output. This kind of information loss is forbidden in the quantum realm. The laws of quantum mechanics demand that information, like energy, must be conserved. A quantum operation can transform a state, but it can never destroy the information that defined it. Every quantum gate is a perfectly reversible rotation, not of a statue, but of a qubit's state vector on the surface of the Bloch Sphere.

This property of reversibility has a profound consequence: any quantum gate can be described mathematically by a special kind of transformation called a unitary matrix. We will spare you the deep dive into linear algebra, but the essential idea behind a unitary transformation is that it preserves the length of a vector. When we apply a quantum gate to a qubit's state vector on the Bloch Sphere, the gate can rotate that vector to any other point on the sphere, but it can never change its length. This is the mathematical guarantee that the vector will always touch the surface of the sphere, ensuring that the probabilities of measuring a 0 or 1 ($|\alpha|^2 + |\beta|^2 = 1$) will always add up to 100%. Quantum gates are the pristine, information-preserving rotations of the quantum world.

Let's meet some of the most important members of this quantum gate family. We'll start with the soloists: the single-qubit gates that operate on one qubit at a time. The most familiar of these is the quantum equivalent of the classical NOT gate, most commonly called the Pauli-X gate. The X-gate does exactly what you'd expect: it flips the state of a qubit. It transforms $|0\rangle$ into $|1\rangle$ and $|1\rangle$ into $|0\rangle$. In our Bloch Sphere model, the X-gate is a 180-degree rotation of the state vector around the x-axis. If the vector is pointing down at the South Pole ($|0\rangle$), a 180-degree rotation around the horizontal x-axis will flip it straight up to the North Pole ($|1\rangle$), and vice-versa.

Next in the Pauli family is the Z-gate. The Z-gate has no direct classical counterpart, and it highlights a uniquely quantum capability: the manipulation of phase. The Z-gate leaves the $|0\rangle$ state completely untouched. However, when it acts on the $|1\rangle$ state, it flips its phase. It turns $|1\rangle$ into $-|1\rangle$. On the Bloch Sphere, this corresponds to a 180-degree rotation around the vertical z-axis. If you are at the South Pole ($|0\rangle$) or the North Pole ($|1\rangle$), a rotation around the axis that passes through them will just spin you in place, leaving your latitude unchanged. For the basis states, this seems to do nothing of consequence, as the probability of measuring a 1 from $|1\rangle$ is the same as from $-|1\rangle$. But as we've discussed, this hidden phase information becomes critically important when qubits interfere with each other. The Z-gate is a vital tool for controlling that interference.

The final member of the Pauli trio is the Y-gate, which, as you might guess, corresponds to a 180-degree rotation around the y-axis of the Bloch Sphere. It performs both a bit flip (like the X-gate) and a phase flip (like the Z-gate) at the same time. The Pauli gates—X, Y, and Z—are the fundamental 180-degree flips of the quantum world, the three cardinal rotations that form a basis for manipulating a qubit's state.

While the Pauli gates are essential, the true superstar of the single-qubit gates, the one that truly unlocks the power of quantum computation, is the Hadamard gate, or H-gate. The Hadamard gate is the primary tool for creating superposition. It is the gate that takes a qubit from a state of classical certainty and places it into a state of quantum potential. If you start with a qubit in the definite state $|0\rangle$ (pointing down on the Bloch Sphere) and apply a

Hadamard gate, it will rotate the state vector up to the equator, transforming it into a perfect 50/50 superposition of $|0\rangle$ and $|1\rangle$. Specifically, it creates the state $(1/\sqrt{2})(|0\rangle + |1\rangle)$.

If you apply the Hadamard gate to a qubit in the $|1\rangle$ state, it also creates an equal superposition, but with a crucial difference in phase: $(1/\sqrt{2})(|0\rangle - |1\rangle)$. The minus sign is a direct result of the phase-flipping nature of rotations. This ability to create different "flavors" of superposition, identical in their measurement probabilities but distinct in their phase, is a key resource for quantum algorithms. The Hadamard gate is our primary mechanism for taking a simple, classical input and expanding it into the vast, parallel workspace of quantum superposition. And because all quantum gates are reversible, applying a second Hadamard gate to a qubit that is in one of these superpositional states will rotate it back to its original definite state. The Hadamard gate both creates and destroys superposition with perfect fidelity.

These single-qubit gates are powerful, but to perform truly complex computations, we need qubits to interact with each other. We need gates that can perform conditional logic, where the state of one qubit affects the operation performed on another. This brings us to the realm of two-qubit gates, the essential duets of the quantum orchestra. By far the most important and widely used of these is the Controlled-NOT gate, or CNOT. The CNOT gate is a cornerstone of quantum computing, a versatile tool used for everything from basic quantum logic to the creation of entanglement.

The CNOT gate operates on two qubits, which we label the "control" qubit and the "target" qubit. The logic is wonderfully simple. If the control qubit is in the state $|0\rangle$, the gate does absolutely nothing to the target qubit. The target qubit passes through unchanged. However, if the control qubit is in the state $|1\rangle$, the gate applies a Pauli-X (a NOT) gate to the target qubit, flipping its state. It is a quantum version of the classical "if-then" statement: IF the control is 1, THEN flip the target.

Let's see what happens when we apply the CNOT to classical basis states:

- If the input is $|00\rangle$ (control is 0, target is 0), the control is 0, so nothing happens. The output is $|00\rangle$.
- If the input is $|01\rangle$ (control is 0, target is 1), the control is 0, so nothing happens. The output is $|01\rangle$.
- If the input is $|10\rangle$ (control is 1, target is 0), the control is 1, so the target is flipped. The output is $|11\rangle$.
- If the input is $|11\rangle$ (control is 1, target is 1), the control is 1, so the target is flipped. The output is $|10\rangle$.

This behavior is useful, but the true power of the CNOT is revealed when we feed it superpositions. This is where the magic of entanglement is born. Let's walk through the most famous recipe in quantum computing: the creation of a Bell state. We start with two qubits, both initialized in the $|0\rangle$ state. Our system is in the simple state $|00\rangle$.

First, we apply a Hadamard gate to the first qubit (our control qubit). This puts it into the superposition $(1/\sqrt{2})(|0\rangle + |1\rangle)$. Since the second qubit is untouched, the state of the entire two-qubit system is now $(1/\sqrt{2})(|00\rangle + |10\rangle)$. Notice that the two qubits are not yet entangled; they are in a simple superposition of two states. The first qubit is in a mix of 0 and 1, while the second qubit is definitely 0.

Now, we apply the CNOT gate, using the first qubit as the control and the second as the target. The CNOT operation acts on both parts of the superposition simultaneously. For the first part of the state, $|00\rangle$, the control qubit is 0, so nothing happens. For the second part of the state, $|10\rangle$, the control qubit is 1, so the target is flipped, changing it to $|11\rangle$. The final result is the state $(1/\sqrt{2})(|00\rangle + |11\rangle)$.

Take a moment to look at this resulting state. This is one of the Bell states we discussed previously. It describes a system in a superposition of two possibilities: either both qubits are 0, or both are 1. You will never find them in a mixed state like 01 or 10. The fates of the two qubits are now inextricably linked. If you measure the first and find it to be 0, you know with absolute certainty that the second is also 0. If you find the first to be 1, the second must also be 1. With a simple two-gate sequence—a Hadamard followed by a CNOT—we have taken two independent qubits and woven them together into a single, spooky, entangled entity. This simple circuit is the fundamental building block for harnessing the power of entanglement in quantum algorithms.

The CNOT is the most common controlled gate, but the principle can be generalized. You can create a Controlled-Z gate (CZ), which applies a Z-gate to the target only if the control is 1, or any other controlled version of a single-qubit gate. These controlled operations are the primary way in which information is shared and correlated between qubits in a quantum computer, forming the essential connections in the computational network.

With this collection of gates—the single-qubit rotations like the Pauli gates and the Hadamard, and a two-qubit entangling gate like the CNOT—we arrive at a remarkable and powerful conclusion. It turns out that you do not need an infinite number of different quantum gates to perform any conceivable quantum computation. Just as the single classical NAND gate is "universal" for classical computing (meaning any other logic gate can be constructed from combinations of NAND gates), a small, finite set of quantum gates is universal for quantum computing.

It has been proven that any possible quantum algorithm, any arbitrary rotation of a state vector in the vast multi-qubit space, can be approximated to any desired degree of accuracy using only single-qubit gates and the CNOT gate. This is a spectacular result. It means that the seemingly infinite complexity of quantum computation can be broken down into a finite sequence of these elementary operations. The challenge of building a quantum computer is not one of inventing new and exotic gates for every problem. The challenge is to physically build high-fidelity versions of these universal gates and to string them together into meaningful sequences. These gates are the LEGO bricks of the quantum world. The next step is to learn how to click them together.

CHAPTER EIGHT: Building Quantum Circuits: Assembling the Pieces

We have now assembled our cast of characters. We have met the qubit, the quantum world's versatile protagonist, capable of holding a spectrum of possibilities within its state. We have also been introduced to the quantum gates, the fundamental verbs of our new computational language, which allow us to rotate, flip, and entangle our qubits with surgical precision. These are the LEGO bricks of the quantum age. The next logical step, and the subject of this chapter, is to become an architect. It is time to take our collection of bricks and begin building with them. It is time to learn how to construct a quantum circuit.

A quantum circuit is, in essence, a quantum program. It is the instruction manual that tells a quantum computer exactly what to do with its qubits, and in what order. Just as a musical score guides an orchestra through a symphony, a quantum circuit diagram lays out a precise sequence of operations, or gates, to be applied to a register of qubits over time. It is a visual language, an elegant and standardized blueprint that allows physicists and computer scientists to design, analyze, and communicate their quantum algorithms. Learning to read these diagrams is the first step toward understanding the practical mechanics of quantum computation.

At first glance, a quantum circuit diagram looks a bit like a musical staff. It is a set of parallel horizontal lines, with time flowing from left to right. Each of these lines represents the life of a single qubit in the computer. We typically label them on the left, starting from the top with $|q_0\rangle$, then $|q_1\rangle$, $|q_2\rangle$, and so on. The state of the qubit at any point in time can be imagined as traveling along this "quantum wire." By convention, we almost always assume that our qubits begin their journey on the far left of the circuit in the initialized state of $|0\rangle$. This is our clean slate, the blank canvas upon which our quantum computation will be painted.

The actions in our program, the quantum gates, are represented by symbols placed directly on these qubit wires. A gate symbol on a wire means that the corresponding operation is applied to that qubit at that specific moment in the computation. A single-qubit gate, like a Hadamard or a Pauli-X gate, is drawn as a box containing the letter that represents it (e.g., an 'H' for Hadamard, an 'X' for a Pauli-X). When we see a box labeled 'H' on the wire for $|q_0\rangle$), it is a clear instruction: "At this point in time, apply a Hadamard gate to the first qubit."

Multi-qubit gates are what connect these parallel lives, allowing our qubits to interact. The most common of these, the CNOT gate, has a special and intuitive representation. It is drawn as a vertical line connecting the control qubit's wire to the target qubit's wire. On the control qubit's wire, we place a solid black dot ($\bullet$), and on the target qubit's wire, we place a larger circle with a plus sign inside ($\oplus$). This diagram beautifully illustrates the gate's logic: the dot on the control line is the "if," and the circle on the target line is the "then flip." This visual connection is what turns a set of independent qubits into a coordinated, and potentially entangled, system.

Finally, at the very end of the circuit, on the far right, we find the act of measurement. This is the moment we extract the classical information that is the result of our computation. Measurement is typically represented by a symbol that looks like a small meter dial or a box with a line pointing from the qubit wire to a parallel classical wire, often drawn as a double line. This signifies the collapse of the qubit's superposition into a definite classical bit, a 0 or a 1, which is then stored in a classical register for us to read. A quantum circuit, then, is the complete story of a computation, from its initial classical state, through its journey of quantum evolution via gates, to its final classical output.

To make this concrete, let's build our very first quantum circuit. We will create a visual blueprint for the process we described at the end of the last chapter: the creation of an entangled Bell state. This is the "hello, world" of quantum circuits, a simple yet profoundly important two-qubit program. We start with two qubit wires, $|q_0\rangle$ and $|q_1\rangle$, both initialized to the $|0\rangle$ state. The state of our combined system at the beginning of the circuit, at "time zero," is simply $|00\rangle$.

The first step in our recipe is to create superposition. To do this, we place a Hadamard gate on the top wire, $|q_0\rangle$. After this gate, $|q_0\rangle$ is transformed from the definite state $|0\rangle$ into the superposition $(1/\sqrt{2})(|0\rangle + |1\rangle)$. The second qubit, $|q_1\rangle$, has not been touched, so it remains in the $|0\rangle$ state. At this intermediate point in our circuit, the total state of our two-qubit system is $(1/\sqrt{2})(|0\rangle + |1\rangle) \otimes |0\rangle$, which expands to $(1/\sqrt{2})(|00\rangle + |10\rangle)$. Note the $\otimes$ symbol, which represents a "tensor product," a mathematical way of combining the states of individual qubits into a single system state. For now, you can simply think of it as a way of distributing the terms, just like in regular algebra.

The second and final step is to create the entanglement. We now apply a CNOT gate. We place the control dot ($\bullet$) on the top wire, $|q_0\rangle$, and the target symbol ($\oplus$) on the bottom wire, $|q_1\rangle$, connected by a vertical line. This gate now acts on the superposition we just created. The CNOT examines the state of $|q_0\rangle$ for each part of the superposition. In the first term, $|00\rangle$, the control qubit is 0, so the gate does nothing. In the second term, $|10\rangle$, the control qubit is 1, so the gate flips the target qubit, changing $|10\rangle$ into $|11\rangle$. The final state of our system, after this two-gate sequence, is $(1/\sqrt{2})(|00\rangle + |11\rangle)$. We have successfully constructed the circuit that generates one of the famous Bell states. In just two simple steps, we have taken two independent, classical-like qubits and woven them into a single, spooky entity.

This process of tracking the quantum state through the circuit, one gate at a time, is the fundamental method for analyzing how a quantum algorithm works. It allows us to follow the intricate transformations of the probability amplitudes and phases, seeing how the state evolves from a simple input to a complex superposition designed to solve a problem. Of course, for a circuit with many qubits, the mathematical description of the state can become enormous very quickly. A ten-qubit system is described by a state with 2^{10}, or 1024, probability amplitudes. This is precisely why simulating a quantum computer on a classical computer is so difficult; writing down and tracking the quantum state is a task that scales exponentially.

Let's look at a slightly more complex and famous example to see how these building blocks can be combined to achieve something truly remarkable: the circuit for quantum teleportation. This circuit demonstrates a fascinating interplay between quantum gates, entanglement, and classical communication. The goal of this protocol is for one person, let's call her Alice, to transmit an unknown quantum state of a single qubit to another person, Bob, who may be far away. She doesn't know what the state is, and she can't simply measure it, as that would destroy the very information she wants to send.

The circuit requires three qubits. The first, $|q_0\rangle$, is Alice's qubit, holding the unknown state $|\psi\rangle = \alpha|0\rangle + \beta|1\rangle$ that she wants to teleport. The other two qubits, $|q_1\rangle$ and $|q_2\rangle$, start as an entangled Bell pair, created using the Hadamard-CNOT circuit we just designed. Alice holds $|q_1\rangle$, and Bob holds $|q_2\rangle$. The first part of the teleportation circuit, then, is the preparation of this entangled resource.

Now for the teleportation itself. Alice wants to transfer the state of $|q_0\rangle$ to Bob's $|q_2\rangle$. To do this, she interacts her qubit, $|q_0\rangle$, with her half of the entangled pair, $|q_1\rangle$. The circuit diagram shows her first applying a CNOT gate, where $|q_0\rangle$ is the control and $|q_1\rangle$ is the target. Then, she applies a Hadamard gate to $|q_0\rangle$. This sequence of operations has the effect of entangling her original qubit with the already-entangled pair, creating a complex, three-qubit entangled state. The specific details of the math are quite involved, but the conceptual result is that the information of her original state, $|\psi\rangle$, is now spread across the correlations of all three qubits.

The next step is for Alice to measure her two qubits, $|q_0\rangle$ and $|q_1\rangle$. In the circuit diagram, we would see the measurement symbols on her two wires. She will get two classical bits as a result, either 00, 01, 10, or 11. This measurement collapses the three-qubit superposition. The amazing part is that depending on which of the four possible classical results Alice gets, Bob's qubit, $|q_2\rangle$, which has been sitting untouched far away, is instantly projected into one of four possible states. Each of these four states is very closely related to the original state $|\psi\rangle$ that Alice wanted to send; they are just rotated versions of it.

The final part of the circuit is classical. Alice must now send her two classical bits of measurement information to Bob over a conventional communication channel, like a phone call or an email. This information is the key that allows Bob to unlock the original state. The last part of the circuit diagram shows two "classically controlled" gates acting on Bob's qubit, $|q_2\rangle$. If Bob receives the message "10" from Alice, for example, the circuit instructs him to apply a Pauli-X gate to his qubit. If he receives "11," he might apply a Z-gate followed by an X-gate. For each of the four possible messages from Alice, there is a unique "correction" operation that Bob must perform. After he applies the prescribed gate, the state of his qubit, $|q_2\rangle$, will be transformed into a perfect replica of Alice's original state, $|\psi\rangle$. The teleportation is complete. The original quantum state has been destroyed at Alice's end and perfectly recreated at Bob's.

This example illustrates a crucial point: quantum circuits are often hybrid quantum-classical systems. They involve purely quantum operations (like Hadamard and CNOT gates), quantum measurements that bridge the quantum-classical divide, and classical logic that processes the measurement results and influences subsequent quantum operations. This synergy is a hallmark of many advanced quantum algorithms.

As we begin to design more complex circuits, it becomes useful to have metrics to describe them, much like we describe classical computer chips by their clock speed or number of cores. In quantum computing, two of the most important metrics are the circuit's "width" and its "depth." The width of a circuit is simply the number of qubits it uses—the number of horizontal wires in the diagram. A circuit with 50 qubits is wider than one with 10. The width determines the size of the computational state space; as we know, N qubits provide a space with 2^N dimensions.

The depth of a circuit is a measure of its execution time. It is defined as the longest path of gates in the circuit from input to output. More simply, you can think of it as the number of time-steps required to execute all the gates, assuming you can perform multiple gates simultaneously on different qubits if they don't overlap. A circuit with a long sequence of gates on a single qubit will have a greater depth than a circuit where many gates are applied in parallel across different qubits. A circuit's depth is the number of layers of computation it contains.

These concepts of width and depth are not just abstract measures of complexity; they are of critical practical importance in the current era of quantum computing. The physical qubits that exist in laboratories today are fragile and highly susceptible to noise and errors from their environment. This phenomenon, known as decoherence, causes the delicate quantum state to decay over time, corrupting the computation. This means that we are in a race against time whenever we run a quantum circuit. The deeper the circuit—the longer it takes to run—the more likely it is that decoherence will destroy our results before the computation is finished.

Consequently, a huge amount of research in quantum computing is focused on finding ways to make circuits as shallow as possible. Quantum computer scientists and software developers work to find clever ways to compile complex algorithms into the shortest, most efficient sequence of gates, minimizing the circuit's depth. This is analogous to a classical programmer optimizing their code to run as fast as possible. In the quantum world, this optimization is not just about performance; it is often the difference between a calculation that works and one that dissolves into random noise.

The circuits we have discussed here—the Bell state creator and the teleportation protocol—are fundamental subroutines, small building blocks that appear as components within much larger and more complex quantum algorithms. The famous algorithms we will encounter in the coming chapters, such as Shor's algorithm for factoring numbers and Grover's algorithm for searching, can be expressed as quantum circuits. They are, in essence, just much wider and deeper versions of the diagrams we have explored here, composed of the very same elementary single-qubit rotations and two-qubit CNOT gates.

A quantum algorithm for factoring a 2048-bit number, for instance, would be a circuit of immense width and depth, requiring thousands of logical qubits and millions, or even billions, of gates. While constructing such a machine is a monumental engineering challenge for the future, the logical blueprint for it is already understood. The language of quantum circuits gives us a clear and unambiguous way to describe that calculation. It is the framework upon which our understanding of quantum computation is built, translating abstract mathematical ideas into a concrete sequence of physical operations, a step-by-step guide for manipulating the quantum world.

CHAPTER NINE: Quantum Algorithms: The Rules of the Quantum Game

We have spent the last several chapters gathering the components for a revolution. We have the foundational particle, the qubit, with its uncanny ability to hold multiple possibilities in superposition. We have the verbs of this new language, the quantum gates, which allow us to manipulate these qubits with the precision of a master watchmaker. And we have the grammar, the structure of the quantum circuit, which provides a blueprint for assembling these operations into a coherent program. We have, in essence, built a quantum workshop. The natural question now is: what do we build? What is the strategy for using these strange and powerful tools to solve a problem?

This is the domain of the quantum algorithm. If a classical algorithm is a recipe, a step-by-step list of deterministic instructions, then a quantum algorithm is more like a piece of music. It is a carefully composed score designed to orchestrate the subtle interplay of probability amplitudes and phases. The goal is not to march toward an answer, but to create a wave of computation that, through a crescendo of interference, washes away every wrong solution and leaves the correct one standing alone on the shore. Learning to "think quantum" requires a fundamental shift away from the sequential logic we are used to and toward this new paradigm of probabilistic choreography.

Let's begin with a simple contrast. Imagine you are given a massive library and tasked with finding a specific book that has been hidden on one of the shelves. The classical approach is straightforward and laborious. You start at the first shelf, check the first book, then the second, then the third, and so on, methodically working your way through the entire library until you find the one you're looking for. This is a brute-force search. It is guaranteed to work, but if the library is large enough, it could take a lifetime.

The quantum approach to a problem like this is entirely different. It does not gain its advantage by simply checking the books faster. Instead, it leverages its unique tools to gain a more holistic understanding of the problem space. A quantum algorithm doesn't "look" at the books one by one. It begins by creating a vast superposition that represents *all* the books in the library simultaneously. It then uses a clever quantum trick to subtly "nudge" the universe in a way that amplifies the possibility of finding the correct book. It is less like a librarian and more like a psychic who, instead of searching, simply gets a "feeling" about where the solution lies.

This general approach, this strategic framework for solving a problem quantumly, can be broken down into a recurring pattern, a kind of universal playbook for many quantum algorithms. While the specific details vary dramatically from one algorithm to the next, the core philosophy remains surprisingly consistent and can be viewed as a sequence of distinct phases.

The first phase is **Initialization**. This is the most straightforward step. We begin by preparing a register of qubits in a known, simple, classical state. By convention, this is almost always the state where every qubit is set to zero: $|00\ldots0\rangle$. This provides a reliable baseline, a clean slate from which the computation can begin. It is the quantum equivalent of clearing a calculator's memory before starting a new problem, ensuring that our results are not influenced by any previous calculations.

The second phase is the great leap into the quantum realm: **Creating Superposition**. This is where the true power of quantum parallelism is unleashed. We typically apply a layer of Hadamard gates to some or all of our qubits. As we saw, a Hadamard gate applied to a qubit in the $|0\rangle$ state transforms it into an equal superposition of $|0\rangle$ and $|1\rangle$. When we do this to a register of N qubits, we create a single quantum state that is an equal superposition of all 2^N possible classical states. We have, in one swift operation, created a computational space that simultaneously represents every possible input to our problem. This is our flooded maze, our library of all possible books.

The third, and arguably most critical, phase is where the problem itself is encoded. This step involves a special kind of quantum subroutine known as an **Oracle** or a "black box." The oracle is a quantum circuit designed to recognize a solution to our problem. Its job is not to tell us the answer, but to "mark" the correct states within our vast superposition. It does this in a uniquely quantum way, typically by manipulating the phase of the probability amplitudes. The oracle acts on our superposition and, for every state that represents a wrong answer, it does nothing. But for any state that represents a correct answer, it multiplies its amplitude by -1, flipping its phase.

This phase-flipping is an incredibly subtle act. It does not change the probability of measuring that state; the square of its amplitude remains the same. The "solution" state is now hidden in plain sight, camouflaged from a direct measurement. It's as if the oracle has attached a tiny, invisible magnetic tag to the correct answer within the sea of possibilities. You can't see the tag, but its presence will fundamentally alter how the state behaves in the next step. The design of this oracle is the art of quantum programming; it is the part of the algorithm that must be custom-built for the specific problem you are trying to solve.

The fourth phase is the grand finale of the quantum part of the computation: **Amplification and Interference**. Having marked our solution states with a phase shift, we now need a way to make them visible. This is accomplished by applying another sequence of quantum gates that is designed to transform the hidden phase information into visible amplitude information. This sequence acts like a lens, focusing the probability of the entire system.

This step, often involving a sophisticated transformation like the Quantum Fourier Transform or an "inversion about the mean" operation, choreographs a massive interference pattern. The states whose phase was flipped by the oracle (the solutions) will interfere constructively with each other, their amplitudes adding up and growing larger. All the other states, the ones that were left untouched by the oracle, will interfere destructively, their amplitudes canceling each other out and shrinking toward zero.

This is the moment of truth where our searchlight focuses its beam, brilliantly illuminating the correct answer while plunging all other possibilities into darkness.

The fifth and final phase is the return to the classical world: **Measurement**. After the interference step has done its work, the quantum state of our register has been transformed. It is no longer an equal superposition of all possibilities. Instead, the probability has been carefully shepherded and concentrated onto the states that correspond to the solution. We now perform a measurement on our qubits. Because of the amplification, the probability of the system collapsing to the state representing the correct answer is now extremely high. We read out the classical string of 0s and 1s and, with high confidence, we have our solution.

This five-step playbook—Initialize, Superpose, Mark with an Oracle, Amplify with Interference, Measure—is the conceptual backbone of a significant portion of the quantum algorithms that have been discovered to date. It highlights the fact that a quantum computation is a delicate balance between exploring a vast parallel space and then carefully extracting a single piece of information from it. The power is not just in calculating all the answers at once, but in the clever use of interference to ensure that when we finally look, we see the answer we were looking for.

This strategic approach also helps us understand which types of problems are most amenable to a quantum speedup. Quantum computers are not a universal panacea for all computational woes. They excel at problems that possess a certain kind of hidden structure, a structure that can be efficiently exploited by an oracle and the interference process. These are often problems where the goal is to find a global property of a function, such as its periodicity (the central challenge in factoring) or the location of a specific marked input (the challenge of searching). Problems that are inherently sequential or that require a large amount of input/output, like running a word processor or a web browser, gain no advantage from this quantum playbook.

It is also important to appreciate that not all quantum speedups are created equal. The impact of a quantum algorithm is measured by how much more efficiently it can solve a problem compared to the best known classical algorithm. These advantages generally fall into two broad categories. The first, and most transformative, is an **exponential speedup**. This occurs when the time a classical computer takes to solve a problem grows exponentially with the size of the input, while the quantum computer's time grows only polynomially. These are the "game-changing" algorithms. They can take a problem that is effectively impossible for any conceivable classical computer and make it solvable. Shor's algorithm for factoring large numbers falls into this category, and its discovery is what transformed quantum computing from an academic curiosity into a technology with world-altering potential.

The second, more common category is a **polynomial speedup**. In this case, both the classical and quantum algorithms have runtimes that grow polynomially with the problem size, but the quantum algorithm's polynomial is smaller. The most famous example of this is Grover's search algorithm. For searching an unstructured database of N items, a classical computer requires, on average, N/2 checks. Grover's algorithm can find the item in approximately $\sqrt{N}$ (square root of N) steps. This is a quadratic speedup. While it is not as dramatic as an exponential speedup, it can still be substantial for very large problems, turning a year-long computation into one that takes only a few days.

To achieve these speedups, quantum algorithm designers have developed a set of powerful, general-purpose tools and subroutines, analogous to the standard libraries used in classical programming. One of the most important is the **Quantum Fourier Transform (QFT)**. The classical Fourier transform is a mathematical tool used ubiquitously in science and engineering to decompose a signal into its constituent frequencies. The QFT is its quantum analogue. It is a quantum circuit that can efficiently transform a state from the computational basis (the familiar $|0\rangle$s and $|1\rangle$s) into a "frequency" basis. This makes it an extraordinarily powerful tool for finding hidden periodicities or repeating patterns in a set of data, which is precisely the kind of structure that Shor's algorithm exploits to factor numbers.

Another fundamental toolkit is **Amplitude Amplification**, which is the general principle behind Grover's algorithm. It is a technique that can be used to take any quantum algorithm that finds a solution with some small probability and iteratively boost that probability closer and closer to 100%. Each iteration of the amplitude amplification process performs a clever geometric rotation in the state space, nudging the state vector away from the non-solution states and closer to the desired solution state. It is the core mechanism for turning a faint quantum "maybe" into a near-certain "yes."

Other algorithmic families, such as quantum walks (the quantum version of classical random walks, useful for certain graph problems) and quantum simulation (using a quantum computer to model another quantum system), are also active areas of research, each with its own strategies and rules. These different approaches are not mutually exclusive; a complex quantum algorithm might use the QFT as a subroutine within a larger structure that also employs principles of amplitude amplification.

The rules of the quantum game are, in the end, the rules of quantum mechanics itself. The challenge and the beauty of designing a quantum algorithm lie in finding innovative ways to use these rules—superposition, entanglement, and interference—to our advantage. It requires a new kind of intuition, one that is comfortable with probabilities instead of certainties, and with holistic transformations instead of sequential steps. The algorithms we are about to explore in the following chapters, Shor's and Grover's, are the crown jewels of this new way of thinking, the first spectacular demonstrations of what can be built when we learn to play by the universe's most fundamental rules.

CHAPTER TEN: Shor's Algorithm: Breaking Modern Encryption

There are moments in the history of science that act as a phase transition, when an idea shifts from a theoretical curiosity into a force with the power to reshape the world. For quantum computing, that moment arrived in 1994 at Bell Laboratories in New Jersey. A quiet mathematician and computer scientist named Peter Shor presented a quantum algorithm that, on paper at least, could solve a problem that was considered utterly intractable for even the most powerful supercomputers imaginable. The problem was integer factorization, and in solving it, Shor's algorithm provided the first concrete, earth-shattering glimpse of the quantum world's disruptive potential. It was the first "killer app" for a quantum computer, and its target was the very foundation of modern digital security.

To understand the monumental impact of Shor's algorithm, we first have to appreciate the lock it was designed to pick. Since the 1970s, the security of our digital lives—from banking transactions and online shopping to encrypted emails and secure government communications—has been built upon a clever mathematical trapdoor known as public-key cryptography. One of the most famous and widely used of these systems is called RSA, named after its inventors Rivest, Shamir, and Adleman. The entire security of the RSA system rests on a single, simple-sounding piece of number theory: it is incredibly easy to take two very large prime numbers and multiply them together, but it is punishingly, prohibitively difficult to take their product and figure out what the original two prime numbers were.

Imagine you are given two large prime numbers, say 1,811 and 2,083. With a calculator, or even by hand, you could quickly multiply them to get their product: 3,772,313. Now, imagine the reverse problem. If you were only given the number 3,772,313 and told to find its two prime factors, where would you even begin? You would have to start guessing, trying to divide it by 3, then 5, then 7, then 11, and so on, testing every prime number until you found one that worked. This is essentially what a classical computer has to do. It has to engage in a brute-force search for the correct factors.

This task becomes exponentially harder as the numbers get bigger. The keys used in modern RSA encryption are not four-digit numbers; they are the product of primes that are hundreds of digits long. The resulting number to be factored, the "public key," can be enormous, often 2048 bits long, which corresponds to a number with over 600 decimal digits. For a classical computer, the time required to factor a number of this size is not measured in hours or days, but in eons. The best-known classical algorithms would take a supercomputer billions of years, longer than the current age of the universe, to crack a single 2048-bit RSA key. Our entire global security infrastructure is built on the faith that this computational wall is, for all practical purposes, insurmountable. Shor's algorithm is the quantum battering ram that threatens to bring that wall tumbling down.

The genius of Peter Shor's approach was that he didn't try to build a faster factoring machine. He recognized that a quantum computer's unique strengths were not suited for a head-on brute-force attack. Instead, he devised a brilliant strategy that reframes the problem entirely. The algorithm is a masterful hybrid of classical and quantum computation, a beautiful example of using a quantum device as a specialized co-processor to solve the one impossible piece of a much larger puzzle. The algorithm cleverly transforms the hard problem of factoring into a completely different, but related, problem: finding the period of a function.

What is the "period" of a function? Imagine a repeating wallpaper pattern. If you look at one point in the pattern, say a small flower, and then move to the right, you will eventually see that exact same flower again. The distance you traveled between the first flower and the second is the "period" of the pattern. It's the length of one complete, repeating unit. Many mathematical functions have a similar property. As you feed them different input numbers ($x = 1, 2, 3, \ldots$), their output values ($f(x)$) go through a

69

sequence that eventually repeats itself. The length of this repeating sequence is the function's period.

The first part of Shor's algorithm is a piece of classical number theory, a mathematical sleight of hand that was known long before quantum computers were ever conceived. This part proves that if you can find the period of a very specific type of function, known as a modular exponentiation function, you can use that period to calculate the factors of your large number with very high probability. The classical steps are: pick a random number, check if it shares any factors with the number you want to factor (a quick and easy check), and if not, use it to construct this special periodic function. The heavy lifting of factoring is magically converted into the heavy lifting of period-finding.

This is where the classical computer hits the same old wall. Finding the period of this function is, classically, just as hard as factoring the original number. You would have to calculate the function for many different inputs until you saw the pattern repeat, a process that is, once again, computationally infeasible for the large numbers used in cryptography. The entire problem has been beautifully repackaged, but it remains locked in an unbreakable box. Shor's algorithm is the key because a quantum computer, it turns out, is a period-finding machine of almost supernatural efficiency.

This brings us to the quantum heart of the algorithm, where we follow the playbook we established in the previous chapter. Let's say we want to factor the number N. After the initial classical steps, we have our special function, $f(x)$, and our mission is to find its period, which we'll call 'r'. To do this, we need two sets of qubits, which we'll call the "input register" and the "output register."

First comes **Initialization**. We prepare both registers of qubits in the all-$|0\rangle$ state. The input register needs to be large enough to hold the range of numbers we want to check for the period. If N is a 2048-bit number, our input register will need a similar number of qubits. This is a significant hardware requirement, but for now, we'll assume we have them.

Second, we **Create Superposition**. This is the classic quantum opening move. We apply a Hadamard gate to every single qubit in the input register. If our input register has 'n' qubits, this single operation creates a state that is an equal superposition of every integer from 0 to 2^n-1. Our quantum computer is now simultaneously considering every possible input to our function. It is holding a state that represents a vast landscape of possibilities, a shimmering cloud of every number we might want to test.

Third, we call upon the **Oracle**. Now we have to perform the actual computation. We need a quantum circuit that takes the value from the input register, let's call it 'x', and computes our special function, $f(x)$, storing the result in the output register. This quantum circuit is the "oracle" for this problem. When this complex operation is applied to our superpositional state, something remarkable happens. The computation is performed on all the 2^n input values at the same time. The result is a massively entangled state. Each value in the input register's superposition becomes linked, or entangled, with its corresponding functional output in the output register.

Imagine the input register holding a superposition of the numbers 1, 2, 3, 4, 5, 6, and so on. Imagine our function has a period of 4, so that $f(1) = f(5), f(2) = f(6)$, and so on. After the oracle runs, the input state $|1\rangle$ becomes entangled with the output $|f(1)\rangle$. The input state $|5\rangle$ becomes entangled with the output $|f(5)\rangle$. But since $f(1)$ and $f(5)$ are the same, both input states $|1\rangle$ and $|5\rangle$ are now linked to the exact same output value. This is a crucial link. All the inputs that produce the same output are now grouped together in the quantum state.

Now for a subtle but important intermediate step. We perform a measurement, but only on the *output* register. We are not yet trying to find the answer. The purpose of this measurement is to tidy up the state. When we measure the output register, the superposition collapses, and we get some single, random value.

71

Let's say we measure the value 'k'. Because of the entanglement we created, this measurement has a profound effect on the input register. The input register's superposition also collapses, but not to a single value. It collapses into a new, smaller superposition consisting of only those input values 'x' that could have produced our measured output 'k'. Because the function is periodic, this means the input register now holds an equal superposition of a set of numbers that are all separated by the period 'r'. We are left with a state that looks something like $|x_0\rangle + |x_0+r\rangle + |x_0+2r\rangle + \ldots$. We have isolated the periodic pattern.

Fourth, we perform the quantum magic trick: **Interference via the Quantum Fourier Transform (QFT)**. We have a state that contains a repeating pattern, but the period 'r' is hidden within the superposition. The QFT is the perfect tool for this job. As we discussed, the QFT is like a mathematical prism. It takes a state described in the computational basis (our list of numbers) and transforms it into the "frequency" basis. When we apply the QFT circuit to our input register, which holds a state with a perfect periodicity 'r', it creates a massive interference pattern.

The amplitudes of all the different states in the superposition begin to interact. The states that are related to the underlying frequency of our pattern—the period 'r'—will interfere constructively. Their probability amplitudes will add up, becoming large and distinct peaks. All the other states, the ones that do not align with the period, will interfere destructively, their amplitudes canceling each other out and dwindling to zero. The QFT acts like a signal processor, taking our messy, superpositional signal and cleanly extracting its fundamental frequency.

Fifth and finally, we **Measure**. After applying the QFT, the state of the input register is no longer a uniform spread. It has been transformed into a state where only a few outcomes have a high probability of being observed. We now measure the input register. The result we get will be a classical string of 0s and 1s. This resulting number is not, in itself, the period 'r'. However, with very high probability, it will be a number that is a multiple of $2^n/r$.

The final leg of the journey is back in the classical world. We take the measurement result from our quantum computer and feed it into a classical algorithm. This algorithm, known as the continued fractions algorithm, is a well-known and very efficient classical method for taking a fraction (like the one we just found) and finding the best rational approximation for it. From this approximation, we can deduce the period 'r'. The process might have to be repeated a few times with different random numbers to be sure, but each run is incredibly fast. Once we have found the period 'r', we plug it into another simple classical formula, and out pop the two prime factors of N. The lock has been picked.

It is difficult to overstate the importance of this algorithm. It is a complete, end-to-end demonstration of how the bizarre rules of the quantum world can be harnessed to solve a problem of immense practical importance. The algorithm gains its power not by checking factors one-by-one, but by preparing a state that embodies the entire problem space at once and then using the wavelike nature of quantum mechanics to perform a global analysis of that space. The QFT is the key that allows the computer to "see" the repeating pattern of the function all at once, a feat that is impossible for a classical machine which must trudge from one point to the next.

This brings us to the practical reality of the situation. Shor's algorithm is proven to work, and it has been successfully demonstrated on quantum computers for factoring very small numbers, like 15 into 3 x 5, and 21 into 3 x 7. These are toy problems, proofs of principle that test the underlying quantum circuits on a small scale. The chasm between factoring 21 and factoring a 2048-bit number is, at present, unimaginably vast. To break a 2048-bit RSA key, it is estimated that a quantum computer would need several thousand perfect, error-free logical qubits and would need to execute a circuit with many millions, or even billions, of gates.

The quantum computers that exist today are still in what is known as the Noisy Intermediate-Scale Quantum (NISQ) era. They have a relatively small number of qubits (from dozens to a few hundred), and those qubits are "noisy," meaning they are highly susceptible to errors and decoherence, which corrupt the computation. Building a fault-tolerant quantum computer of the scale required to run Shor's algorithm on a cryptographically relevant number is one of the single greatest scientific and engineering challenges of our time. It will require breakthroughs in qubit stability, control, and, most importantly, the implementation of robust quantum error correction.

Nevertheless, the blueprint exists. The mathematical threat is no longer hypothetical. The discovery of Shor's algorithm ignited a new field of research known as post-quantum cryptography, a global effort by mathematicians and computer scientists to develop new encryption standards that are secure against attacks from both classical and quantum computers. These new methods are based on different mathematical problems that are believed to be hard even for a quantum computer to solve. The race is on to upgrade our global security infrastructure before a sufficiently large quantum computer becomes a reality. Shor's algorithm was a warning shot, a clear signal that the age of quantum computation would not just bring new tools for science and discovery, but also profound new challenges to the stability and security of our digital world.

CHAPTER ELEVEN: Grover's Algorithm: The Quantum Search Engine

In the grand narrative of quantum algorithms, if Peter Shor's masterpiece is the elegant, specialized key designed to pick a single, immensely important lock, then the creation of Lov Grover is the quantum world's answer to the Swiss Army knife. It is a more general, more broadly applicable, yet in some ways more modest tool. Presented in 1996, just two years after Shor's algorithm, Grover's algorithm tackles a problem so fundamental and ubiquitous that we often take it for granted: the problem of search. It offers a solution that is not just clever, but also provides one of the clearest illustrations of how a quantum computer can strategically manipulate probability to its advantage.

Imagine you are handed a phone book for a massive city, but with a terrible twist. The entries are not in alphabetical order. The names and numbers are completely jumbled, a chaotic list of millions of entries with no discernible pattern. Your task is to find the phone number for one specific person, say, John Smith. With no alphabetical structure to guide you, what can you do? You have no choice but to start at the beginning, check the first name, see if it's John Smith, and if not, move on to the second, then the third, and so on. This is the essence of an unstructured search. You are looking for a needle in a haystack, and your only strategy is to pick up every single piece of hay until you find it.

For a classical computer, this is the end of the story. If your phone book has N entries, you might get lucky and find John Smith on the first try. You might also be incredibly unlucky and find him in the very last entry, requiring N checks. On average, you can expect to perform N/2 checks to find your target. For computer scientists, this is known as a search with a time complexity of O(N), meaning the time it takes to solve the problem grows in direct, linear proportion to the size of the haystack. There is no classical trick, no clever shortcut, that can do better. The lack of structure is an absolute barrier.

Grover's algorithm provides a way to leap over this barrier. It doesn't offer an exponential speedup like Shor's algorithm did for factoring; it can't take a task that would last for the age of the universe and reduce it to a few hours. Instead, it offers a quadratic speedup. Grover's algorithm can find the needle in the N-item haystack in a number of steps that is proportional to the square root of N, or $O(\sqrt{N})$. This may sound less dramatic than an exponential leap, but the practical implications are enormous.

Consider our phone book with one million entries. A classical search would, on average, require 500,000 checks. Grover's algorithm could accomplish the same task in about $\sqrt{1,000,000}$, which is only 1,000 steps. For a database with a trillion entries, the classical machine would need 500 trillion checks on average, a task that would take a modern supercomputer months or years. Grover's algorithm would need only about $\sqrt{1,000,000,000,000}$, or one million steps, a task that could potentially be completed in seconds. It turns a prohibitively long search into a manageable one. It is a fundamental improvement on the very nature of searching.

So how does it work? Grover's algorithm is a perfect student of the quantum playbook we outlined earlier. It follows the core strategy of using superposition to create a vast parallel workspace and then using interference to amplify the signal of the correct answer. The algorithm is a repeating loop, a rhythmic quantum pulse that, with each beat, pumps more and more probability into the state that represents the solution.

Let's walk through the process. Suppose our database has N items. To represent these, we need a register of n qubits, where 2^n is at least as large as N. We can then associate each of the N items with a unique quantum state, from $|00...0\rangle$ to the state representing N-1. One of these states, let's call it $|w\rangle$ for "winner," is the item we are searching for.

The first two steps are by now familiar. We **Initialize** our qubit register to the all-zero state, $|0...0\rangle$. Then, we **Create Superposition** by applying a Hadamard gate to every qubit. This creates a state, which we'll call $|s\rangle$, that is a uniform superposition of all 2^n possible basis states. At this point, the amplitude of every single state is equal. The probability of measuring any one state is the same as any other. It's a perfectly flat, democratic distribution of probability. Our quantum state represents every entry in the phone book at once, but with no preference for any of them.

Now comes the custom-built component, the **Oracle**. For Grover's algorithm, the oracle is a quantum circuit that knows how to recognize the winning state $|w\rangle$. Its job is not to tell us what $|w\rangle$ is, but to subtly "mark" it within the superposition. It does this with a conditional phase shift. When the oracle is applied to our uniform superposition $|s\rangle$, it checks every state in that superposition. For every state that is *not* the winner, it does nothing. For the single state that *is* the winner, $|w\rangle$, it flips its phase by multiplying its amplitude by -1.

Let's visualize this. Imagine the amplitudes of all the states in our superposition are represented by the height of bars on a graph. Initially, all the bars are at the same positive height. After we apply the oracle, all the bars remain at that height, except for one. The bar corresponding to our winning state, $|w\rangle$, is now flipped, pointing downwards to the same negative height. This is a clever, subtle move. If we were to measure the state right now, this phase flip would be completely invisible. The probability of measuring a state depends on the square of its amplitude, and the square of a positive number is the same as the square of its negative counterpart. The winning state is marked, but it's still hidden, like a note written in invisible ink.

The next step is the ingenious core of the algorithm, the **Amplification** phase. This is where the invisible ink is revealed. This part of the circuit is often called the Grover diffusion operator, and its job is to amplify the amplitude of the marked item. It does this through a beautiful geometric trick known as "inversion about the mean." The process works as follows: first, the circuit calculates the average amplitude of all the states in the current superposition. Then, for each state, it inverts its amplitude relative to that average. If a state's amplitude was a certain amount *above* the average, it is moved to be the same amount *below* the average. If it was below the average, it's moved to be above it.

Let's see what this does to our state. After the oracle's phase flip, the amplitude of our winner $|w\rangle$ is large and negative, while all the other N-1 states have small, positive amplitudes. This means the average amplitude of all the states is a very small positive number, just slightly above zero. Now we apply the inversion. All the "wrong" states, whose amplitudes were slightly above this tiny average, are flipped to be slightly below it. Their amplitudes are slightly reduced. But our winning state, $|w\rangle$, which had a large negative amplitude far below the average, is flipped to a new position far *above* the average. Its amplitude is dramatically increased. In one fell swoop, we have taken a tiny bit of probability from every wrong answer and funneled it into the right one. The winning state, which started off just like everyone else, now stands head and shoulders above the crowd.

This sequence of two operations—the oracle's phase flip and the diffusion operator's inversion about the mean—constitutes one single "Grover iteration." We haven't found the answer yet, but we have significantly boosted its probability. So, we do it again. We apply the oracle a second time, which flips the now-large positive amplitude of $|w\rangle$ back to being large and negative. Then we apply the diffusion operator again, which performs another inversion about the new average, pumping the amplitude of $|w\rangle$ even higher.

This can be visualized as a rotation in a two-dimensional plane. Imagine one axis represents the winning state $|w\rangle$, and the other axis represents a superposition of all the other "wrong" states. Our initial uniform superposition is a vector that lies almost entirely along the "wrong" axis, with only a tiny component pointing along the "winner" axis. The oracle's phase flip acts like a reflection of this vector across the "wrong" axis. The diffusion operator then acts as a reflection across the line of our initial state vector. The net result of these two successive reflections is a single, clean rotation. With each iteration, we rotate our state vector away from the "wrong" axis and closer and closer toward the "winner" axis.

The final step is, of course, **Measurement**. But when do we measure? We can't just keep iterating forever. It turns out there is an optimal number of times to repeat the process. If we keep rotating our state vector, we will eventually "overshoot" the winner axis, and the probability of measuring the correct state will start to decrease again. The mathematical analysis shows that the optimal number of iterations is approximately $(\pi/4)\sqrt{N}$. After performing this precise number of rotations, the state vector will be pointing almost directly at the winning state, meaning its amplitude is now very close to 1. We then measure the qubit register, and with a probability that is close to 100%, the quantum state collapses to our desired answer, $|w\rangle$.

Grover's algorithm is a beautiful example of a probabilistic algorithm being carefully controlled to produce a nearly deterministic outcome. It doesn't find the answer by learning where it is, but by systematically destroying the possibilities of it being anywhere else. It's a process of elimination on a grand, quantum scale.

The applications of this powerful searching tool extend far beyond simple database lookups. Any problem that can be solved by a brute-force search can, in principle, be sped up quadratically by Grover's algorithm. This includes a wide class of notoriously difficult problems in computer science known as NP-complete problems. These are problems, like the Traveling Salesman Problem, for which no efficient classical algorithm is known. While Grover's algorithm doesn't make these problems "easy"—a quadratic speedup on an exponential problem still results in an exponential problem—it could extend our reach, allowing us to solve instances of these problems that are currently just beyond our classical grasp.

It can also be used for cryptographic purposes, though its impact is less severe than that of Shor's algorithm. For example, it can be used to speed up attacks on symmetric encryption systems like AES by reducing the complexity of a brute-force key search from $O(N)$ to $O(\sqrt{N})$. To counteract this threat, security experts simply recommend doubling the key length. For instance, a 128-bit key, which has 2^{128} possible combinations, is as resistant to a Grover-based attack as a 256-bit key is to a classical attack. This is a manageable and well-understood defense.

There are, as always, practical caveats. The power of Grover's algorithm is most pronounced when the "database" is not a physical list of items stored in memory, but is rather the output of a function that can be computed. The process of building an oracle that has to query a classical hard drive for each item in a superposition would be so slow that it would likely erase any quantum advantage. The algorithm truly shines when we are trying to invert a function—that is, finding an input x that produces a specific output y from a function f(x). In this case, the oracle can be constructed as a quantum circuit that computes f(x) and flags the state where the output matches y.

Furthermore, like all quantum algorithms, Grover's algorithm requires a fault-tolerant quantum computer to run for large values of N. Each Grover iteration is a complex sequence of quantum gates, and the accumulation of errors over many iterations is a significant challenge for the noisy, intermediate-scale quantum computers of today. The number of qubits required grows with the size of the database, and the depth of the circuit grows with the square root of its size.

Despite these challenges, Grover's algorithm remains a cornerstone of the field. It was the second great example of a quantum algorithm that could definitively outperform a classical one, proving that the quantum advantage was not a one-trick pony limited to the specific structure of factoring. It demonstrates a more general principle of amplitude amplification, a technique that has since become a fundamental tool in the quantum algorithm designer's toolkit. It shows how a quantum computer can "feel" its way toward a solution, not by looking at the details, but by manipulating the global properties of a vast, interconnected quantum state. It is, in the truest sense, a quantum search engine.

CHAPTER TWELVE: The Hardware of the Quantum Age: Building a Quantum Computer

For the past several chapters, we have been living in a pristine, idealized world. We have been architects of the mind, drawing elegant circuit diagrams where perfect qubits dance through flawless gates, their superpositions and entanglements holding firm until the final, revelatory measurement. In this abstract realm of mathematics and logic, a quantum computer is a powerful and beautiful thing. Now, however, we must leave this clean room of theory and descend into the messy, noisy, and often frustratingly difficult world of physical reality. It is time to ask the fundamental question: how do you actually build one of these machines?

The answer, in short, is with extreme difficulty. Building a functional, large-scale quantum computer is arguably one of the most formidable scientific and engineering challenges ever undertaken by humanity. It is a task that pushes the limits of material science, cryogenics, electronics, and precision control. It is not simply a matter of designing a new kind of microchip. It is a holistic challenge of building a new kind of universe, a tiny, isolated pocket of reality where the fragile rules of quantum mechanics can be shielded from the disruptive clamor of the classical world, yet still be precisely controlled and measured. A quantum computer is not a single device; it is a complex and sprawling ecosystem of supporting hardware, a life-support system for the quantum states at its heart.

To bring some order to this immense challenge, it is helpful to have a set of ground rules, a checklist of essential properties that any aspiring quantum computing hardware must possess. In the year 2000, the physicist David DiVincenzo laid out a set of five such criteria that have since become a guiding framework for the entire field. These "DiVincenzo Criteria" are the quantum computer builder's equivalent of a master chef's essential ingredients. Lacking any one of them will result in a machine that is, at best, an interesting physics experiment rather than a functional computer.

The first and most obvious criterion is the need for a **scalable physical system with well-characterized qubits**. This is the fundamental requirement for a stage and actors. You need to have an actual, physical thing—be it an atom, an electron, a photon, or a tiny superconducting circuit—that can serve as your qubit. This physical system must have two distinct and controllable quantum states that can represent our familiar $|0\rangle$ and $|1\rangle$. But it's not enough to have just one. The system must be "scalable," meaning you have a clear physical path to building systems with not just a handful, but hundreds, thousands, and eventually millions of these qubits working in concert. Furthermore, they must be "well-characterized," which means we must understand their properties with incredible precision. We need to know their energy levels, how they respond to external stimuli, and how they interact with their neighbors.

The second criterion is **the ability to initialize the state of the qubits to a simple fiducial state**. Before any symphony begins, the orchestra must first fall silent. Similarly, before any quantum computation can start, we must be able to reliably reset all of our qubits to a known, simple starting point. By convention, this is the all-zero state, $|00\ldots0\rangle$. This is a non-trivial engineering task. For many types of qubits, the $|0\rangle$ state corresponds to their lowest possible energy level, or "ground state." Achieving this state of computational purity often involves actively cooling the system to extraordinarily low temperatures to drain away thermal energy, and then using precise laser or microwave pulses to nudge any stray qubits down into this ground state. Without a reliable reset button, the results of one computation would bleed into the next, rendering the machine chaotic and useless.

This leads us to the third, and perhaps most difficult, criterion: **long relevant decoherence times, much longer than the gate operation time**. This is the battle against the quantum computer's arch-nemesis, decoherence. As we have touched upon, quantum states like superposition and entanglement are exquisitely fragile. They exist in a delicate conversation with the universe. The slightest unwanted interaction—a stray photon, a tiny vibration, a fluctuation in a nearby magnetic field—can be enough to disrupt this conversation, causing the quantum state to "decohere" and collapse into a boring, classical state. Decoherence is the constant, ticking clock that threatens to destroy our computation before it is finished.

The "coherence time" is a measure of how long a qubit can maintain its quantum integrity. A gate operation, such as a Hadamard or CNOT gate, also takes a certain amount of time to perform. DiVincenzo's third rule states that your qubit's coherence time must be vastly longer than the time it takes to perform a single gate. If it takes you one microsecond to flip a qubit, but your qubit can only hold its superposition for half a microsecond, you will never be able to complete even the simplest operation. The goal is to be able to perform thousands, or even millions, of gate operations within the coherence lifetime of your qubits. The entire art of quantum hardware design is a relentless war against decoherence, a quest to build a sanctuary so quiet that the quantum whispers are not drowned out.

The fourth criterion brings us back to our circuit diagrams: the need for a **"universal" set of quantum gates**. It's not enough to have stable qubits; we must be able to manipulate them. We need a physical mechanism to serve as our puppeteer's strings, allowing us to perform the precise rotations that constitute our quantum gates. We need the physical equivalent of a Hadamard gate to create superposition, and a CNOT gate to generate entanglement. For different types of qubits, these "strings" take different forms. For trapped ions, they are precisely timed laser pulses. For superconducting qubits, they are carefully shaped microwave pulses. Whatever the method, we must be able to implement a universal gate set, the collection of fundamental operations from which any quantum algorithm can be built. This control must be executed with incredibly high fidelity; a "sloppy" gate that doesn't perform the exact intended rotation will quickly introduce errors that cascade through the computation.

Finally, the fifth criterion is the need for a **qubit-specific measurement capability**. At the end of our computation, after all the gates have been run, we need to read out the answer. This means we must have a reliable method to measure the final state of each individual qubit, forcing its collapse to either a 0 or a 1. This measurement must be accurate, and it must be possible to perform it on a specific qubit without accidentally disturbing the states of its neighbors before they can be measured themselves. This is akin to trying to listen to the whisper of a single person in a crowded library without causing anyone else to look up. The physical techniques for this are as varied as the qubits themselves, involving everything from detecting the fluorescence of an atom to measuring the tiny change in frequency of a microwave resonator.

These five criteria provide a powerful lens through which to view the anatomy of a real quantum computer. When you see a picture of a quantum computing system, you are not just looking at a single processor. You are looking at a massive, complex machine, where each component is dedicated to satisfying one or more of these demanding conditions. The centerpiece, the star of the show, is the Quantum Processing Unit, or QPU. This is the "chip" itself, a small, intricate device, often only a few square centimeters in size, where the physical qubits reside. The QPU is a marvel of microfabrication, a precisely engineered landscape designed to house and control quantum phenomena.

The QPU, however, cannot operate in a vacuum. It is controlled by a vast and complex array of classical hardware, the **Control and Measurement System**. This is the machine's nervous system. It consists of racks of high-frequency electronics—microwave signal generators, arbitrary waveform generators, and digitizers—that create the precise pulses needed to execute quantum gates. These pulses are sent down a series of specially designed, shielded cables into the heart of the machine, where they manipulate the qubits. The same system is also responsible for capturing the faint signals that come back out during measurement and translating them into the classical bits that form the answer. A quantum computer is, in this sense, a fundamentally hybrid device, a quantum core that is inextricably linked to and controlled by a sophisticated classical brain.

Perhaps the most visually striking and physically imposing part of a modern quantum computer is the apparatus designed to create the **Extreme Environment** required for the qubits to survive. This is the life-support system, and its primary job is to satisfy DiVincenzo's third criterion by fighting decoherence with every tool at its disposal. The two main enemies in this fight are thermal energy (heat) and electromagnetic noise. To combat heat, many leading quantum computers, particularly those using superconducting qubits, are housed inside a device called a dilution refrigerator.

These refrigerators are magnificent, multi-layered constructions that often resemble a golden, inverted chandelier. They use a complex process involving the circulation of helium isotopes to achieve temperatures that are almost incomprehensibly cold. A typical operating temperature for a superconducting QPU is around 15 millikelvin, which is about -273.135 degrees Celsius. This is more than 100 times colder than the average temperature of deep space. This extreme cold is necessary to bring the qubits into their quantum ground state and to quell the storm of thermal vibrations that would otherwise instantly destroy any delicate superposition. Each layer of the "chandelier" is a progressively colder thermal shield, designed to intercept and remove heat before it can reach the QPU nestled at the very bottom.

To combat the second enemy, electromagnetic noise, the entire system is encased in a series of shields. Just as a recording studio is soundproofed, a quantum computer must be "electromagnetically" proofed. A layer of high-permeability metal, often a nickel-iron alloy called mu-metal, is used to shield the system from stray magnetic fields, including the Earth's own. The entire apparatus is also designed to be isolated from physical vibrations, sometimes being built on dedicated concrete pads or using sophisticated active damping systems. The goal is to create a bubble of absolute stillness and silence, an environment so pristine that the only things the qubits can "hear" are the deliberate control signals sent by the scientists.

Even with all this technology, we confront another monumental hurdle as we try to grow our machines: the **Interconnect Challenge**. A small, ten-qubit processor might be manageable, but how do you wire up and control a processor with one million qubits? For every qubit, you need one or more dedicated control lines running from the room-temperature electronics down through the various cooling stages of the refrigerator to the QPU. The complexity and heat load of this "I/O" problem quickly becomes a bottleneck. Researchers are actively developing new technologies to address this, such as cryogenic control chips that can sit next to the QPU in the cold environment, and even exploring photonic (light-based) interconnects to shuttle quantum information between different parts of a processor or even between different quantum computers.

This entire stack of hardware, from the cloud-based software interface where a user writes their code down to the individual atoms or circuits at the bottom of a refrigerator, represents the **Quantum-Classical Interface**. A user today does not typically sit in front of the quantum computer itself. Instead, they interact with it through the cloud. They write a program using a software development kit like IBM's Qiskit or Google's Cirq, which translates their desired quantum circuit into a sequence of low-level pulse commands. This sequence is then sent to the control hardware at the laboratory, which executes the experiment on the QPU. The classical measurement results are then sent back to the user over the internet.

Building a quantum computer, then, is a symphony of extremes. It requires the coldest temperatures, the quietest environments, the highest vacuums, and the most precise control signals we can muster. Each component, from the dilution refrigerator to the microwave generator to the QPU itself, is a masterpiece of engineering in its own right. The challenge lies in making all these disparate, cutting-edge technologies work together in perfect harmony to coax a small patch of the universe into performing a computation that is unlike anything that has come before. The path from the theoretical elegance of a quantum algorithm to its practical execution is paved with these immense, but not insurmountable, hardware challenges.

CHAPTER THIRTEEN: Trapped Ions, Superconductors, and Photonics: Types of Qubits

The qubit, as we have come to know it, is a beautiful and powerful abstraction. It is a point on a sphere, a delicate blend of alpha and beta, a perfect quantum entity. But to build a computer, we must tether this abstract idea to the physical world. A qubit cannot exist as a mere concept; it must have a body, a physical home where its quantum state can be nurtured, controlled, and ultimately measured. The quest to build a quantum computer is, in many ways, a quest to find the perfect physical host for a qubit. The challenge is that the very properties that make a system quantum— its isolation, its fragility—also make it incredibly difficult to work with.

As it turns out, there is no single, universally agreed-upon "best" way to build a qubit. The field of quantum hardware is a vibrant and fiercely competitive landscape of different approaches, each with its own unique set of strengths, weaknesses, and fanatical adherents. It is a technological Cambrian explosion, with researchers exploring a menagerie of quantum systems, from the atomic to the artificial. In this chapter, we will take a tour of the three leading contenders in this race: the patient and precise trapped ion, the fast and flexible superconductor, and the fleet-footed but elusive photon. These are not just different engineering solutions; they are fundamentally different philosophies about how to tame the quantum world.

Our first stop is the domain of the trapped ion, a favorite of physicists who appreciate elegance and precision. The approach here is beautifully straightforward: if you want a perfect, reliable quantum system, why not start with the one that nature has already perfected for you? The qubit in this platform is a single atom. Specifically, it is an ion—an atom, such as ytterbium or calcium, that has had one of its outermost electrons gently removed. This leaves the atom with a net positive electric charge, which is the key to the entire scheme. An electrically charged particle, unlike a neutral one, can be grabbed and held in place by electromagnetic fields.

Imagine an impossibly small cage whose bars are not made of steel, but of oscillating electric fields. This is an ion trap. Inside this cage, a single ion can be levitated in an almost perfect vacuum, suspended in space and isolated from the noisy outside world. This pristine isolation is a trapped ion's superpower. With nothing to bump into, its delicate internal quantum states can survive for an astonishingly long time. The coherence times for trapped-ion qubits are the envy of the quantum computing world, often measured not in microseconds or milliseconds, but in seconds or even minutes. In the frantic, fast-paced world of quantum operations, this is an eternity.

The qubit itself is not the entire atom, but two of its internal electronic energy levels. Just as electrons in an atom can only exist in specific orbits, or energy states, we can select two of these stable states to serve as our $|0\rangle$ and $|1\rangle$. Often, these are "hyperfine" energy levels, which are incredibly stable and well-defined, making the ion a near-perfect quantum clock. To manipulate the qubit—to perform a single-qubit gate—scientists take aim at the trapped ion with a precisely tuned laser beam. By controlling the frequency, phase, and duration of the laser pulse, they can drive the qubit's state vector to any desired point on the Bloch Sphere with extraordinary accuracy. The fidelity of these single-qubit gates is among the highest achieved for any qubit platform.

Creating entanglement between two ions is a more subtle and beautiful dance. The ions in the trap, being positively charged, naturally repel each other. This electrical repulsion links them together into a delicate, crystalline structure. They behave like a set of tiny marbles connected by invisible springs. This shared, collective vibration is the communication channel, the "quantum bus," that allows the qubits to talk to each other. A carefully aimed laser pulse on one ion can be used to "pluck" this shared string of motion. This vibration, or "phonon," can then be felt by a second ion, influencing its internal state. A carefully choreographed sequence of laser pulses on two different ions can thus create a CNOT gate, weaving their quantum states together into an entangled pair. A key advantage here is that this bus is fully connected; in principle, any ion in the chain can be made to interact with any other, a powerful feature for running complex algorithms.

When the computation is complete, reading out the answer is also accomplished with lasers. A different laser is shone on the ion, one that is tuned to interact with only one of the two qubit states, say the $|1\rangle$ state. If the ion is in the $|1\rangle$ state, it will absorb the laser light and then re-emit it as a shower of photons, glowing brightly. A sensitive camera, like the sensor in a high-end digital camera, captures this fluorescence. If the ion is in the $|0\rangle$ state, it will ignore the laser and remain dark. The result is a simple, high-contrast binary measurement: light means 1, dark means 0.

The trapped-ion approach offers a compelling list of advantages. The qubits are made by nature, so they are perfectly identical and stable. Their coherence times are exceptionally long, and the fidelity of their gate operations is world-class. However, this platform is not without its challenges. The primary drawback is speed. The process of using the shared vibrational motion for two-qubit gates is inherently slow, with gate times measured in microseconds. While the qubits may live for minutes, a slow clock speed limits the number of operations you can perform within that lifetime. Scaling up is another significant hurdle. Managing long, one-dimensional chains of ions becomes difficult, and controlling the vast array of individual laser beams required for a large processor is a formidable engineering challenge.

If trapped ions are the meticulous, patient watchmakers of the quantum world, then our next candidates, superconducting qubits, are the industrial titans. This is the approach favored by tech giants like Google and IBM, and it stems from a completely different philosophy. Instead of borrowing a perfect quantum system from nature, the idea here is to build one from scratch, to engineer an "artificial atom" on a silicon chip using the same fabrication techniques that created the classical computing revolution. This approach sacrifices the pristine perfection of a natural atom for the speed, flexibility, and potential scalability of semiconductor manufacturing.

A superconducting qubit is not an atom at all; it is a tiny electrical circuit, a microscopic loop of metal like aluminum or niobium, patterned onto a chip. When this circuit is cooled down to temperatures colder than deep space, just a few thousandths of a degree above absolute zero, the metal becomes a superconductor. In this state, electricity flows without any resistance, and the collective behavior of the electrons in the circuit begins to obey the laws of quantum mechanics. Just like a real atom, this man-made circuit has discrete, quantized energy levels. The lowest energy state, the "ground state," is designated as our $|0\rangle$, and the next level up, the first "excited state," becomes our $|1\rangle$.

The magic ingredient that makes this all possible is a tiny device called a Josephson junction. This is essentially a very thin layer of insulating material sandwiched between two superconductors. It acts as a non-linear inductor, which is a fancy way of saying it ensures that the energy "rungs" on our circuit's ladder are not evenly spaced. This is crucial, as it allows us to isolate the $|0\rangle$ and $|1\rangle$ states and treat them as a qubit, without accidentally exciting the circuit to higher energy levels. The most common type of superconducting qubit, the "transmon," has been carefully engineered to be particularly insensitive to background noise.

Control in this world is not about lasers, but about microwaves. The qubit chip is mounted at the bottom of a dilution refrigerator and connected via a series of coaxial cables to a room full of complex microwave electronics. To perform a single-qubit gate, a precisely shaped microwave pulse, lasting only a few nanoseconds, is sent down the cable. The frequency of this microwave signal is tuned to perfectly match the energy gap between the $|0\rangle$ and $|1\rangle$ states. This resonant pulse drives the qubit's state around the Bloch Sphere. Two-qubit gates are performed by physically connecting two of these artificial atoms on the chip, often with a small capacitor or another tunable coupling element. This connection allows the state of one qubit to influence the energy levels of the other, and another carefully timed set of microwave pulses can execute a CNOT or other entangling operation.

Measurement is also done via microwaves. Each qubit is coupled to its own tiny microwave resonator, a sort of on-chip tuning fork. The resonant frequency of this tuning fork is slightly different depending on whether the qubit it's listening to is in the $|0\rangle$ state or the $|1\rangle$ state. To read out the qubit, a weak microwave signal is sent to the resonator, and the signal that reflects back is captured and analyzed. By measuring the phase and amplitude of this reflected signal, scientists can determine the resonator's frequency and, by extension, the state of the qubit.

The primary advantage of the superconducting platform is speed. Gate operations are incredibly fast, typically taking only tens of nanoseconds. This allows for many more operations to be performed within the qubit's coherence time. Furthermore, the ability to use established semiconductor fabrication techniques offers a promising path to scaling up to chips with thousands or even millions of qubits. However, this artificial nature is also the source of its main weakness. Because the qubits are manufactured, they are not perfectly identical. Each one has slight imperfections, and they are much more sensitive to noise from the surrounding solid-state environment. Their coherence times, while constantly improving, are still orders of magnitude shorter than those of trapped ions. They are also prisoners of their physical layout; a superconducting qubit can typically only interact with its immediate neighbors on the chip, limiting the connectivity that is essential for some algorithms.

Our final leading platform takes us into a completely different realm of physics. It trades the static, stationary qubits of ions and circuits for "flying qubits" made from the fundamental particles of light itself: photons. Photonic quantum computing is a paradigm built around manipulating and measuring single photons as they travel through a network of optical components, like a quantum Rube Goldberg machine.

In this approach, the qubit information is encoded into a property of the photon. The most common choice is polarization, the direction in which the photon's electromagnetic field oscillates. For example, a horizontally polarized photon can represent $|0\rangle$, and a vertically polarized photon can represent $|1\rangle$. Thanks to superposition, a photon can also exist in a diagonal polarization, representing a mix of both states. Single-qubit gates are remarkably simple to implement. A standard optical device called a wave plate, when placed in the photon's path, can rotate its polarization with high precision, effectively performing any desired rotation on the Bloch Sphere.

Measurement is also a strong suit for photonics. A polarizing beam splitter is a crystal that acts as a traffic cop for light, directing horizontally polarized photons down one path and vertically polarized photons down another. By placing hyper-sensitive single-photon detectors at the end of each path, we can perform a perfect measurement. If the top detector "clicks," the photon was vertical ($|1\rangle$); if the bottom one clicks, it was horizontal ($|0\rangle$).

The great nemesis of photonic quantum computing, the monumental challenge that has defined the field for decades, is the two-qubit gate. The problem is simple: photons, by their very nature, do not interact with each other. Two beams of light can pass right through one another without noticing the other is there. This is great for coherence—photonic qubits are incredibly robust against environmental noise—but it makes conditional logic seem almost impossible. How can you make one photon's state affect another's if they refuse to talk?

The solution is a clever trick based on quantum interference. If you send two identical photons into the two input ports of a special mirror called a beam splitter at exactly the same time, they will interact. Due to a purely quantum phenomenon known as the Hong-Ou-Mandel effect, the two photons will always stick together and leave through the same output port. By building complex networks of these beam splitters and other optical components, it is possible to construct a probabilistic CNOT gate. The gate doesn't always work, but when it does, it heralds its own success with a specific pattern of detector clicks. This means that photonic quantum computers must be built with a large amount of redundancy and error correction to overcome the inherent randomness of their entangling operations.

Photonics offers a unique set of trade-offs. Its qubits are extremely coherent and can operate at room temperature, eliminating the need for bulky dilution refrigerators. They are also the natural choice for quantum communication, as quantum information can be sent over long distances using existing fiber-optic networks. The main disadvantages are the extreme difficulty of building reliable two-qubit gates and the challenge of creating perfect, on-demand sources of single photons.

These three platforms—trapped ions, superconductors, and photons—are the current front-runners, but the race is far from over. Other promising contenders are gaining ground, each with a unique physical insight. Neutral atoms, held in arrays of optical "tweezers," behave much like trapped ions but may be easier to scale. Quantum dots, tiny semiconductor crystals that act as artificial atoms, offer a potential bridge between the worlds of superconducting circuits and photonics. And on the far horizon lies the tantalizing prospect of topological qubits, a radically different approach where information is encoded in the very fabric of a material's structure, making it theoretically immune to local noise. The final winner in this technological marathon is far from certain. It may even be that the future of quantum computing is a hybrid one, where different types of qubits are used for different tasks—superconducting circuits for fast processing, and photonic links for communication—all working together in a complex and powerful ecosystem.

CHAPTER FOURTEEN: The Challenge of Noise: Taming the Quantum World

Imagine you are a master spy, attempting to exchange a vital secret with a fellow agent across a crowded ballroom. The secret is encoded in a series of incredibly subtle gestures—a slight nod, a particular blink, the precise angle of a held teacup. To communicate successfully, you require a clear line of sight and absolute silence between you. Now, imagine that just as you begin, the orchestra strikes up a deafening crescendo, strobe lights begin to flash, and a panicked crowd starts jostling you from all sides. Your subtle gestures are lost in the chaos. The message is scrambled, the meaning destroyed. This, in a nutshell, is the daily predicament of a quantum computer. The subtle, secret conversation is the quantum computation, and the deafening, chaotic ballroom is the ever-present classical environment.

In the pristine world of our circuit diagrams, qubits live in a perfect, silent vacuum. In reality, they are prisoners of a relentless and noisy world. The central, overwhelming challenge in building a functional quantum computer is not a conceptual one—we have the algorithms and the blueprints—but a practical one. It is the monumental task of shielding our fragile quantum states from the constant, disruptive chatter of their surroundings. This ever-present, unwanted interaction between a quantum system and its environment is known collectively as quantum noise, and the process by which this noise strips a qubit of its "quantumness" is the dreaded phenomenon of decoherence.

Decoherence is the arch-villain in our quantum story. It is the force that constantly seeks to drag the strange, superpositional world of the qubit back into the boring, predictable reality of a classical bit. A qubit in a superposition of $|0\rangle$ and $|1\rangle$ is not in a stable equilibrium. It is in a highly delicate, artificial state that requires extreme isolation to maintain. The universe, it seems, has a strong preference for classical certainty. Decoherence is the mechanism by which it enforces this preference. It is a slow, inexorable leak, where the precious quantum information held in the qubit's state seeps out into the wider environment, becoming hopelessly scrambled and lost. The "coherence time" of a qubit is a measure of how long it can resist this process before its quantum identity is erased. For a quantum computation to succeed, it must complete its entire sequence of operations long before this clock runs out.

This hostile noise is not a single entity, but a hydra-headed monster with sources both inside and outside the machine. One of the most fundamental sources is thermal energy. As we saw in Chapter Twelve, leading quantum computers are cooled to temperatures colder than deep space. This is done to combat the constant jiggling of atoms that we call heat. Even at 15 millikelvin, however, there is still a residual whisper of thermal energy. This can manifest as tiny vibrations in the chip or stray particles of energy, called phonons, traveling through the substrate. If one of these stray energy packets happens to bump into a qubit that is in the excited $|1\rangle$ state, it can be enough to cause it to spontaneously relax down to the $|0\rangle$ ground state. This type of error, known as amplitude damping, is a direct loss of information.

Another pervasive enemy is electromagnetic noise. Our world is awash in a sea of electromagnetic fields, from radio stations and Wi-Fi signals to the Earth's own magnetic field. A quantum computer is an exquisitely sensitive antenna, and these stray fields can be picked up by the qubits and their control wiring. A fluctuating magnetic field, for instance, can cause the energy gap between a qubit's $|0\rangle$ and $|1\rangle$ states to wobble slightly. This, in turn, causes the phase of the qubit to precess or drift in an unpredictable way. This process, known as phase damping or dephasing, is particularly insidious. It doesn't cause the qubit to flip from $|1\rangle$ to $|0\rangle$, but it erodes the delicate phase relationships that are the lifeblood of quantum interference.

The noise is not just coming from the outside; the call is also coming from inside the house. The very equipment we use to control the qubits is itself a significant source of error. The laser and microwave pulses used to perform quantum gates are generated by classical electronics, which are not perfect. A pulse that is meant to rotate a qubit by exactly 90 degrees might, in reality, rotate it by 89.9 degrees due to a tiny calibration error. A pulse that is supposed to have a perfect rectangular shape might have slight distortions. These small imperfections, known as control errors, accumulate with every gate that is applied, causing the qubit's state to slowly drift away from its intended trajectory on the Bloch Sphere.

As we try to scale up our processors by packing more and more qubits onto a chip, another gremlin appears: crosstalk. Qubits, by design, need to be able to talk to their neighbors to perform two-qubit gates. The challenge is to make sure they stop talking when they are supposed to. Crosstalk occurs when an operation on one qubit unintentionally affects the state of another. Imagine sending a microwave pulse intended for qubit A, but a small amount of that signal leaks over and gives a little "nudge" to its neighbor, qubit B. This unwanted nudge can corrupt qubit B's state, introducing an error into a part of the computer that was supposed to be idle. This problem becomes exponentially harder to solve as qubits get closer together and their wiring becomes more complex.

Even the final act of measurement is fraught with peril. The signals we extract from a qubit to determine if it is a 0 or a 1 are often incredibly faint. These signals must be amplified and processed by a chain of classical electronics, and this process is susceptible to its own forms of noise. A measurement error occurs when, for instance, a qubit is truly in the $|1\rangle$ state, but the detection system incorrectly reports it as a $|0\rangle$. High-fidelity measurement is a critical component of any quantum computer, as even a perfect computation is useless if you cannot read the answer correctly at the end.

The cumulative effect of these various noise channels on a quantum algorithm can be catastrophic. Let's consider the impact on our two most important quantum resources. First, superposition. The whole idea of quantum parallelism rests on the ability to prepare a register in a superposition of a vast number of states. Decoherence attacks this directly. An amplitude damping error can cause a qubit to fall out of superposition prematurely, effectively removing a whole swath of possibilities from the computational space. The quantum computer, which was supposed to be exploring a million paths at once, might suddenly find that half its paths have vanished.

The corruption of phase information is even more devastating. Quantum algorithms like Shor's are essentially large-scale interference experiments. They are designed to choreograph a precise cancellation of all the wrong answers, leaving only the right one. This depends on maintaining exact phase relationships between all the 2^N states in the superposition. Phase damping acts like a random, unpredictable shuffling of these phase relationships. It is like trying to produce a perfect musical chord while each musician randomly shifts the timing of their note. The harmony is lost, the destructive interference fails to cancel, the constructive interference fails to build, and the final measurement yields a result that is essentially random noise.

Perhaps the most dangerous aspect of quantum noise is its ability to propagate. In a classical computer, a "bit-flip" error in one part of the memory is generally a local problem. It stays where it is. In a quantum computer, thanks to the magic of entanglement, an error on a single qubit can quickly spread to infect the entire system. Imagine we have two qubits in an entangled state. If a random phase error strikes the first qubit, its state is corrupted. Now, if we apply a CNOT gate using that first qubit as the control, the error doesn't just stay there. The CNOT operation will propagate that phase error to the target qubit, entangling the error itself with the state of the second qubit. A single, local error has now become a correlated, two-qubit error. In a complex algorithm with many entangling gates, a few small errors early on can cascade into an avalanche of garbage across the entire quantum register.

Given the severity of this problem, it is essential for scientists to have a clear and standardized way to measure and talk about it. We need a way to grade our quantum hardware. One of the most fundamental metrics for this is **fidelity**. Fidelity is a measure of "how close" a real-world quantum operation is to the ideal, perfect operation described by the mathematics. We can speak of the fidelity of a single-qubit gate, a two-qubit gate, or a measurement. It is usually expressed as a percentage. A CNOT gate with 99% fidelity sounds pretty good, but in the context of a quantum algorithm that might require millions or billions of gates, it's a disaster. Even a tiny error of 0.1% per gate can quickly accumulate to the point where the final result is completely wrong. The holy grail for building a fault-tolerant quantum computer is achieving gate fidelities of 99.9% or, ideally, 99.99% and beyond.

While fidelity tells us about the quality of our individual components, it doesn't give us a complete picture of a quantum computer's overall power. A computer with a million noisy qubits might be less powerful than one with fifty very clean, high-fidelity qubits. To capture this trade-off between quantity and quality, a more holistic benchmark called **Quantum Volume (QV)** was developed. Quantum Volume attempts to measure the largest, most complex quantum circuit that a machine can successfully run. It asks, what is the largest "square-shaped" circuit (where the number of qubits equals the number of time-steps, or depth) a computer can execute with reliable results? A computer that can run a 6-qubit, 6-step-deep circuit is said to have a Quantum Volume of 2^6, or 64. To achieve a high QV, a machine must have not only enough qubits, but also low error rates, good connectivity between qubits, and accurate control systems. It is a much more practical measure of a computer's true computational capability in the face of noise.

The relentless battle against noise has led to a two-pronged strategy. The first, and most practical for today's machines, is the field of **quantum error mitigation**. This is a collection of clever software and programming tricks designed to work around the noise, rather than eliminate it. The core idea of mitigation is to accept that every run of your circuit will be noisy, but to try to estimate the effect of that noise and subtract it out from your final answer. One popular technique is called zero-noise extrapolation. Here, you would run your quantum circuit not once, but multiple times, and for each run, you intentionally amplify the noise by a known amount. By plotting the noisy results against the known noise levels, you can then extrapolate backward to predict what the result would have been in the ideal, zero-noise case. These techniques are essential for getting useful results from the machines of today, but they are ultimately just a clever patch. They don't fix the underlying problem, and they don't scale to the truly massive computations of the future.

The ultimate, long-term solution, and the subject of our next chapter, is **quantum error correction (QEC)**. This is a far more ambitious and powerful idea, inspired by the error correction codes that are ubiquitous in classical computing. The central concept of QEC is to accept that individual physical qubits will always be noisy. Instead of trying to build a perfect physical qubit, the strategy is to use redundancy. The information of a single, ideal "logical qubit" is encoded across the collective, entangled state of many physical qubits. These physical qubits are then constantly measured in a special way that can detect if an error has occurred on one of them, and importantly, can do so without disturbing the precious logical information itself. If an error is found, a correction operation is applied to put the errant qubit back in its place. This is the grand vision for fault-tolerant quantum computing: building stable, nearly perfect logical qubits out of a sea of noisy physical ones.

This vision, however, remains a distant one. The overhead in terms of the number of physical qubits required to build a single, error-corrected logical qubit is immense, possibly requiring hundreds or even thousands of physical qubits for one logical one. For now, we live in the Noisy Intermediate-Scale Quantum, or NISQ, era. This name, coined by physicist John Preskill, perfectly encapsulates our current reality. We have quantum processors with an "intermediate scale" of qubits—dozens to a few hundred—but they are all "noisy." They are too small and too error-prone to run the massive error correction codes needed for fault tolerance, but they are also becoming too large to be perfectly simulated by even the best classical supercomputers.

The grand challenge for physicists and programmers in the NISQ era is to work within these limitations. The game is to design quantum algorithms that are, on the one hand, powerful enough to potentially show an advantage over classical computers for some specific problem, but on the other hand, are "shallow" enough—meaning they have a low circuit depth—that they can be run to completion before decoherence washes away the result. It is a delicate and fascinating balancing act, a search for a "quantum advantage" in an imperfect world. Taming the quantum world is not about eliminating noise entirely, but about learning to compute within its ever-present, roaring storm.

CHAPTER FIFTEEN: Quantum Error Correction: Keeping Qubits in Line

The previous chapter left us in a rather precarious situation. We have a powerful, revolutionary new form of computation, but it is built upon a foundation of almost unimaginable fragility. Our quantum computer is a virtuoso performer forced to play a priceless Stradivarius in the middle of a hurricane. The constant, chaotic storm of noise from the classical world threatens to knock our delicate quantum states out of tune at every moment, turning our carefully composed computational symphony into a meaningless cacophony. The fight against this noise is the central drama in the story of building a quantum computer.

Thus far, the battle has been one of brute force and isolation. We have built magnificent golden chandeliers to freeze our qubits to near absolute zero, and we have encased them in layers of shielding to create pockets of electromagnetic silence. We are engaged in a heroic engineering effort to build a quieter room. But what if a quieter room is not enough? What if, no matter how hard we try, the hurricane always finds a way to leak through? This is where a profound shift in strategy is required. We must move from a strategy of error prevention to one of error management. We must accept that errors will happen and devise a way to fix them on the fly. This is the domain of quantum error correction (QEC), a field of study so clever and counter-intuitive that it almost feels like magic.

To appreciate the genius of QEC, it is helpful to first look at its classical counterpart. Error correction is a technology that is so deeply embedded in our digital lives that we are almost completely unaware of it. From the way your computer stores data on its hard drive to the way your phone communicates with a cell tower, error correction codes are constantly working in the background, silently fixing the tiny corruptions that are an inevitable part of physical information processing.

The simplest classical idea is the repetition code. If you want to send a single bit of information, say a "0," and you are worried it might get flipped to a "1" by noise, you don't just send "0." You send "000" instead. The receiver at the other end gets the three bits and uses a simple majority vote. If they receive "001," they can be reasonably confident that the second bit was flipped by noise and the intended message was "000," which decodes to "0." By using three physical bits to encode one "logical" bit, we have created a more robust system. This principle of redundancy is the heart of all error correction.

When quantum physicists first considered applying this idea to qubits, they immediately ran into a series of seemingly insurmountable roadblocks, fundamental laws of quantum mechanics that seemed to forbid the very act of error correction. The first and most famous of these is the No-Cloning Theorem. This is a fundamental principle of quantum mechanics which proves, with mathematical certainty, that it is impossible to create an exact, independent copy of an unknown quantum state. You cannot simply take your precious qubit, $\alpha|0\rangle + \beta|1\rangle$, and create two more identical copies to build a $(\alpha|0\rangle + \beta|1\rangle)(\alpha|0\rangle + \beta|1\rangle)(\alpha|0\rangle + \beta|1\rangle)$ state. The quantum world does not have a copy machine. This immediately kills our simple classical repetition code, which relied entirely on making copies.

The second roadblock is the observer effect. Our classical majority vote system relied on looking at the individual bits to see if an error had occurred. But as we know from the core mysteries of quantum mechanics, the moment you measure a qubit in a superposition, you force it to collapse into a definite 0 or 1. The very act of checking for an error would destroy the delicate quantum information—the values of α and β—that you are trying to protect. You cannot check for damage without demolishing the very thing you are guarding.

The third challenge is that the nature of quantum errors is far richer and more complex than a simple bit-flip. In the classical world, an error is a binary event: a 0 becomes a 1 or vice-versa. A qubit, however, can suffer a bit-flip error (an X-gate error), but it can also suffer a phase-flip error (a Z-gate error), which turns $\alpha|0\rangle + \beta|1\rangle$ into $\alpha|0\rangle - \beta|1\rangle$. Worse still, a quantum error is not an all-or-nothing event. A qubit's state vector can be nudged by a tiny, infinitesimal amount in any direction on the Bloch Sphere. There is a continuous infinity of possible errors that can occur, not just two. It seems like an impossible game. You cannot copy your data, you cannot look at your data, and the errors you are trying to fix can come in an infinite variety.

The solution to this seemingly impossible puzzle is one of the most brilliant achievements of quantum information science. It is a way to use redundancy without copying, and a way to detect errors without looking. The core idea is to encode the information of a single, perfect "logical qubit" into the shared, entangled state of several noisy "physical qubits." The information ceases to belong to any one physical qubit. Instead, it is stored non-locally in the intricate web of correlations between them. An error on a single physical qubit might damage one part of this web, but the global information remains intact, protected by the collective.

Let's see how this works with the simplest possible example: a code to protect against a single bit-flip error. We cannot clone our logical qubit, $|\psi\rangle = \alpha|0\rangle + \beta|1\rangle$, but we can cleverly distribute its information across three physical qubits. The encoding process uses a circuit of CNOT gates to transform our initial state into the following three-qubit entangled state: $\alpha|000\rangle + \beta|111\rangle$. This is not a copy. It is a single, new quantum state, often called a Greenberger–Horne–Zeilinger (GHZ) state. The original information, α and β, now describes the superposition of the entire three-qubit system.

Now, suppose a bit-flip error occurs on the first physical qubit. Our pristine state is corrupted, becoming $\alpha|100\rangle + \beta|011\rangle$. The problem is now to detect this error without measuring the data qubits themselves and collapsing the state. This is where the magic happens. We introduce two additional "ancilla" or helper qubits, initialized to $|0\rangle$. We then perform a series of CNOT gates from the data qubits to these ancilla qubits. The first ancilla is used to check the "parity" of the first two data qubits: we perform a CNOT from data qubit 0 to the ancilla, and another from data qubit 1 to the same ancilla. The ancilla will flip to 1 only if the two data qubits are different. We do the same with the second ancilla, using it to check the parity of data qubits 1 and 2.

After this process, we measure only the two ancilla qubits. Let's see what they tell us. In the original, error-free state, all three data qubits are the same (all 0s or all 1s), so both ancillas will read "00." Now consider our corrupted state. The first two data qubits (1 and 0 in the first term, 0 and 1 in the second) are different, so the first ancilla will flip. The second two data qubits (0 and 0, 1 and 1) are the same, so the second ancilla will not flip. The measurement of the ancillas will yield the result "10." This two-bit classical result is called the "error syndrome." It acts like a little diagnostic code.

Notice what has happened. We have learned that an error has occurred, and we have even learned *where* it occurred (the fact that the parity between qubits 0 and 1 is wrong, but the parity between 1 and 2 is right, uniquely identifies qubit 0 as the culprit). Crucially, we have learned all this without gaining any information whatsoever about α and β. The logical state remains safely hidden in its superposition. Once we have the syndrome, the recovery is simple. A syndrome of "10" is the instruction to our control system: "Apply a Pauli-X gate to the first physical qubit." This flips it back, restoring the original encoded state. We have successfully detected and corrected an error without violating any of the fundamental rules of quantum mechanics.

This ingenious three-qubit code handles bit-flips, but what about the equally pernicious phase-flips? The solution is a beautiful demonstration of quantum thinking. It turns out that a phase-flip error is mathematically equivalent to a bit-flip error, but viewed from a different perspective. If you apply a Hadamard gate to a qubit, then a phase-flip occurs, and then you apply another Hadamard gate, the net effect is the same as a single bit-flip. The Hadamard gate effectively transforms one type of error into the other. This gives us a recipe for a three-qubit phase-flip correction code: first, apply a Hadamard to each of your three data qubits. Then, run the exact same bit-flip correction procedure as before. Finally, undo the initial transformation by applying another round of Hadamards. This circuit will now successfully detect and correct a single phase-flip error.

The first true quantum error-correcting code, devised by Peter Shor in 1995, elegantly combined these two ideas. The Shor code uses nine physical qubits to encode a single logical qubit. It essentially wraps the three-qubit bit-flip code inside the three-qubit phase-flip code, creating a nested structure that can protect against any arbitrary single-qubit error, whether it be a bit-flip, a phase-flip, or any superposition of the two. This was a landmark achievement, as it proved for the first time that building a reliable quantum computer in a noisy world was not just a hope, but a theoretical possibility.

Since these early discoveries, the field of QEC has evolved significantly. While the Shor code was a brilliant proof of principle, its overhead of nine physical qubits for one logical qubit, and the complexity of its required gate operations, make it difficult to implement in practice. The modern front-runner for practical quantum error correction, especially for hardware based on 2D chip architectures, is a family of codes known as **surface codes**.

The idea behind the surface code is to arrange the physical data qubits on a 2D grid, like the squares on a chessboard. Interspersed within this grid are the ancilla qubits, which act as our error-detecting probes. The circuit for a surface code is a highly repetitive, rhythmic process. In a continuous cycle, the ancilla qubits interact with their four neighboring data qubits, performing parity checks and generating syndrome information. Each ancilla is like a tiny security guard, constantly patrolling its local four-qubit neighborhood and reporting back if anything looks amiss.

A classical computer continuously monitors the stream of syndrome measurements coming from all the ancillas on the chip. In an error-free world, this stream would be a constant string of zeros. When a quantum error occurs on one of the data qubits, it causes the neighboring ancillas to start reporting "1" instead of "0." These "1"s are like a trail of breadcrumbs, marking the location and time of the error event. The job of the classical "decoder" is to look at this evolving 2D map of syndrome bits and, like a detective solving a crime, deduce the most likely sequence of errors that could have created that pattern. Once it has made its diagnosis, it can update its internal model of the quantum state, effectively correcting the error without ever having to physically touch the qubits again.

This brings us to one of the most important concepts in all of quantum computing: the **fault-tolerance threshold theorem**. This theorem is the light at the end of the long, dark tunnel of quantum noise. It states that if the physical error rate of the individual components of your quantum computer—your gates and measurements—is below a certain critical value, or "threshold," then it is possible to use quantum error correction to suppress the error rate of your logical qubit to be as low as you want. You can achieve this simply by making your error-correcting code larger, for example, by using a bigger grid of qubits in your surface code.

This theorem is our mathematical guarantee that a scalable, reliable quantum computer is physically possible. However, it comes with a monumental price tag. The threshold for the surface code is believed to be around 1%, meaning our physical gates need to have fidelities of at least 99%. While the best systems today are just beginning to cross this crucial line, there is another, even more daunting challenge: the overhead. To achieve a logical qubit with an error rate that is, say, a million times better than the physical error rate might require a surface code consisting of over a thousand physical qubits.

This is the stark reality of the path forward. Building a truly large-scale, fault-tolerant quantum computer—the kind that can run Shor's algorithm on a meaningful number—is not a matter of building a machine with a few thousand qubits. It is a matter of building a machine with millions of high-quality physical qubits, the vast majority of which will not be used for computation itself, but will serve as the support structure for a much smaller number of nearly perfect logical qubits. Quantum error correction is not a minor software patch. It is a complete redesign of our computational architecture, a scheme for building robustness out of fragility, and the only known path to unlocking the true, world-changing potential of the quantum age.

CHAPTER SIXTEEN: Quantum Supremacy and Advantage: Proving the Power

For years, the promise of quantum computing has been a shimmering vision on the horizon, a powerful theoretical idea backed by small-scale laboratory experiments. We have journeyed through the strange physics of the qubit, the elegant logic of quantum gates, and the immense engineering required to build even a rudimentary processor. But this journey inevitably leads to a critical, high-stakes question: How do we know if it's working? How do we prove, in a concrete and undeniable way, that these machines are not just fantastically complex scientific instruments, but are genuinely crossing a threshold into a new computational territory, a place where our trusted classical computers can no longer follow?

This is not a question with a simple answer. It is not like a footrace where the first to cross a clear finish line is the winner. The race between classical and quantum computers is more like a complex, multi-terrain triathlon where the rules and even the length of the course are constantly changing. To bring some clarity to this contest, the scientific community has established a series of grand challenges, monumental milestones that would serve as the signposts on the road to a quantum future. The first, and most intensely debated, of these milestones is a concept known as quantum supremacy.

Quantum supremacy is a term that sounds grand, absolute, and perhaps a little intimidating. In reality, its scientific definition is very precise. It does not mean that a quantum computer is superior at all, or even most, tasks. It refers to the specific, experimental demonstration of a quantum processor successfully performing a single, well-defined computational task that is practically impossible for the most powerful classical supercomputer on Earth to perform in any reasonable amount of time. The key here is that the task does not have to be useful. It doesn't need to cure a disease or break a code. Its sole purpose is to be a computational Everest, a problem deliberately chosen to be easy for a quantum computer but brutally, punishingly hard for a classical one. It is a stress test, a proof of principle designed to show that quantum machines have, in fact, entered a new regime of computation.

For years, this milestone remained a theoretical target. Then, in the autumn of 2019, the world of computing was jolted by a paper published by a team of researchers at Google. They claimed to have reached this pivotal goal. Their experiment, conducted on a 54-qubit superconducting processor named "Sycamore," was a landmark moment, the quantum world's equivalent of the Wright brothers' first flight at Kitty Hawk. It was a brief, highly controlled, and not particularly practical demonstration, but it aimed to prove that powered flight was, in fact, possible.

The task Google's team designed for the Sycamore chip was as esoteric as it was brilliant. It is known as "random quantum circuit sampling." Imagine you have a quantum circuit of a certain size and depth, but instead of a carefully structured algorithm like Shor's, the sequence of quantum gates is chosen randomly. The result of running this circuit is a complex, entangled quantum state spread across all the qubits. If you measure this state, you will get a string of 0s and 1s as an output. Due to the probabilistic nature of quantum mechanics, each time you run the circuit and measure, you will get a different output string.

However, the outputs are not completely random. The specific pattern of random gates creates a subtle interference pattern in the quantum state, making some output strings slightly more likely to appear than others. The result is a highly complex, but predictable, probability distribution. The computational task, then, is this: run the random quantum circuit a few million times, collect the resulting output strings, and verify that your collection of samples accurately reflects the probability distribution predicted by the theory of quantum mechanics. It is the quantum equivalent of being asked to roll a set of intricately loaded dice a million times and then prove that the results you got match the known weightings of the dice.

For the quantum computer, this task is, in a sense, natural. It is what it was born to do. The Sycamore processor, with its 53 functioning qubits, simply had to execute the random circuit and be measured. The process of generating one of these samples took the quantum machine about 200 seconds. The challenge was for a classical computer to do the same thing. To solve this problem classically, a supercomputer has no choice but to simulate the entire quantum circuit. It must calculate the evolution of the full 2^{53}-dimensional quantum state, an impossibly vast mathematical space. It has to track the amplitude and phase of every one of the nine quadrillion basis states as they are transformed by each gate in the circuit.

The Google team calculated that for their specific circuit, this simulation would be an epic undertaking. They estimated that on the world's most powerful supercomputer at the time, IBM's Summit, the task of calculating the probability of just one output string, let alone generating a million samples, would take approximately 10,000 years. A 200-second task for their quantum chip was, they claimed, a 10,000-year task for the mightiest classical machine in existence. This was the basis of their claim to have achieved quantum supremacy.

The announcement sent waves through the scientific and technological communities. It was hailed as a major breakthrough, a clear signal that quantum computing was transitioning from a theoretical science into an experimental reality. However, the story was not that simple. The claim soon drew a sharp and detailed rebuttal from Google's main competitor in the superconducting qubit space, IBM.

The team at IBM did not dispute the experimental results from the Sycamore chip. They agreed that the Google team had successfully built and run their quantum circuit. What they disputed was the 10,000-year classical estimate. The IBM researchers pointed out that Google's estimate was based on a simulation algorithm that assumed the entire quantum state vector had to be stored in the supercomputer's main memory (its RAM). But a machine like Summit is not just a collection of fast processors and RAM; it also possesses a colossal amount of secondary storage in the form of hard disk drives.

IBM proposed a different classical algorithm, one that was much smarter about how it used the computer's resources. Their method would break the problem into smaller pieces and cleverly shuttle data between the fast RAM and the slower, but vastly larger, disk storage. By doing so, they argued, the same task could be completed on Summit not in 10,000 years, but in a mere 2.5 days. While 2.5 days is still significantly longer than 200 seconds, it is a far cry from an impossible timescale.

This counter-argument did not erase Google's achievement, but it brilliantly illustrated a crucial point: the line for quantum supremacy is not a fixed point, but a constantly moving target. As quantum hardware gets better, so do classical algorithms and classical hardware. The contest is a dynamic one, where new ideas on one side can suddenly shift the goalposts for the other. The debate highlighted that claiming supremacy depends not only on how fast your quantum computer is, but also on how clever the best classical programmers are.

The controversy also sparked a conversation about the term "supremacy" itself. Many in the field found the word to be misleading and unnecessarily triumphalist. It suggests a general superiority, when in reality, the demonstration was for one highly contrived and specifically chosen problem. Furthermore, the term carries historical and social baggage that many researchers found uncomfortable. As a result, many now prefer alternative phrases like "quantum primacy" or, more commonly, have shifted their focus to the next, more meaningful milestone on the roadmap: quantum advantage.

If quantum supremacy is about proving a quantum computer can be the best in the world at an abstract, potentially useless task, then quantum advantage is about proving it can be the best at a genuinely useful one. Quantum advantage is the point at which a quantum computer can solve a real-world problem of scientific or commercial value faster, cheaper, or more accurately than any known classical method. This is the promised land that researchers, governments, and investors are truly seeking. This is the point where quantum computers stop being scientific curiosities and start creating tangible economic and societal impact.

Achieving quantum advantage is, in many ways, a much harder and more nuanced challenge than achieving supremacy. The problems are not of our own design; they are dictated by the needs of science and industry. A useful problem in drug discovery might involve simulating the complex structure of a molecule, while a problem in finance might require optimizing a vast investment portfolio. To show an advantage, a quantum computer must outperform not just a single, brute-force simulation algorithm, but the entire toolkit of highly optimized, specialized classical heuristics and approximation methods that have been developed over decades to tackle these very problems.

For example, a quantum algorithm for optimizing a logistics network would need to find a better route than the best existing classical software that companies like FedEx or Amazon already use. That classical software is the product of many years of research and is already exceptionally good. Proving a quantum advantage means clearing a very high bar of real-world performance. It is the difference between building a concept car that can break a land-speed record in the salt flats and building a production car that is more fuel-efficient and reliable for a daily commute than anything else on the market.

While the Google experiment was the first to grab the headlines, the quest to demonstrate a clear computational advantage is an ongoing global effort. In 2020 and 2021, teams of researchers in China, led by Jian-Wei Pan, announced their own supremacy-style experiments using a completely different type of hardware: photonic quantum computers. Their machines, named Jiuzhang, were designed to solve a different, but similarly contrived, sampling problem known as Gaussian Boson Sampling. Their results were equally impressive, claiming to have performed a calculation in minutes that would take a classical supercomputer billions of years. These experiments confirmed that the phenomenon was not limited to one type of hardware or one specific problem, reinforcing the fundamental principle that certain computational tasks are natively better suited to quantum mechanics.

These early supremacy experiments are best viewed not as an end, but as a beginning. They are the first definitive experimental evidence that the theoretical models of quantum computation are correct and that it is possible to build and control a quantum system large enough to venture beyond the boundaries of classical simulation. They are a powerful validation of the entire field, a signal that the immense investment and effort are leading toward a genuinely new computational paradigm. They proved that quantum mechanics, when harnessed on a sufficient scale, can produce a statistical complexity that classical systems struggle to replicate.

The ultimate goal, however, remains quantum advantage. The focus of the field is now shifting from these carefully constructed benchmark problems to tackling challenges with more immediate relevance. Researchers are now designing and running experiments on today's noisy, intermediate-scale quantum (NISQ) devices that aim to approximate the ground state energies of small molecules for chemistry, or to find approximate solutions to optimization problems. These experiments are not yet demonstrating a definitive advantage, but they are the crucial first steps in learning how to map real-world problems onto quantum hardware and in benchmarking the performance of these machines against classical methods.

The path from here is a gradual one. It is unlikely that there will be a single, dramatic moment when quantum advantage is declared for all problems. Instead, we are likely to see a slow, creeping advance, where quantum computers first show a small advantage for a very specific, niche scientific problem. Then, as the hardware improves and the algorithms become more sophisticated, that beachhead of advantage will expand to include more complex problems in fields like materials science, then perhaps finance, and eventually, medicine. The journey from Kitty Hawk to the Boeing 747 was a long one, filled with countless incremental improvements and technological breakthroughs. The journey from Sycamore to a universally useful quantum computer will be a similar story of patient, persistent progress.

CHAPTER SEVENTEEN: The NISQ Era: Working with Imperfect Quantum Computers

We stand at a peculiar and exhilarating moment in the history of computation. The grand vision of a fully fault-tolerant quantum computer, a machine capable of running vast algorithms like Shor's with near-perfect logical qubits, remains a distant, shimmering goal on the horizon. Yet, in laboratories around the world, the first generation of genuine quantum processors has been born. These are not the flawless, idealized machines of our circuit diagrams. They are temperamental, fragile, and profoundly imperfect. Welcome to the NISQ era, a term coined by the physicist John Preskill that has come to perfectly define our current reality: we are working with Noisy, Intermediate-Scale Quantum computers.

Let's break down that acronym, for it contains the three defining characteristics of our age. The "N" stands for Noisy. As we have seen, our physical qubits are locked in a constant battle with their environment. They are buffeted by thermal vibrations, rattled by electromagnetic fields, and prone to errors from imperfect control signals. This noise is not a minor inconvenience; it is the central, defining feature of these machines. They lack the sophisticated error-correcting codes that will one day provide a shield of invincibility. Any computation we run is in a race against the clock of decoherence, a constant struggle to finish before the delicate quantum state dissolves into meaningless static.

The "IS" stands for Intermediate-Scale. Today's processors have moved beyond the single-digit qubit counts of early experiments. We now have machines with dozens, hundreds, and in some roadmaps, thousands of qubits. This is a critical sweet spot. These machines are, for certain specific tasks, becoming too large and complex to be simulated efficiently by even the world's most powerful classical supercomputers. We have crossed a threshold into a new territory. However, they are still far too small to accommodate the immense overhead required for full quantum error correction. They are intermediate: powerful enough to be interesting, but not yet powerful enough to be perfect.

Finally, the "Q" for Quantum. This is the most important part. Despite their flaws, these are not mere curiosities. They are true quantum devices, capable of harnessing the strange and powerful resources of superposition and entanglement. The challenge, and the entire focus of this era, is to figure out what, if anything, we can do with this new and unruly beast. How do we extract a meaningful "quantum advantage" from a machine that is simultaneously powerful and flawed? It is a question that has forced a complete rethinking of how we design quantum algorithms, pushing us toward a new paradigm of pragmatic, hybrid computation.

The central constraint of the NISQ era is the problem of circuit depth. Every quantum gate we apply takes time and introduces a small amount of error. As our quantum circuits get longer, or "deeper," these errors accumulate, and the chance that decoherence will destroy our result increases. The grand algorithms like Shor's require circuits of immense depth, with billions of sequential gates. These are completely out of reach for NISQ hardware. The algorithms of today must be "shallow." They must be designed to achieve their goal in the smallest number of computational steps possible, completing their work in a short, intense burst before the quantum state inevitably degrades.

This severe limitation has given rise to the dominant strategy of the NISQ era: the hybrid quantum-classical approach. Instead of trying to solve an entire problem on the quantum processor, we treat the QPU as a specialized co-processor, a unique piece of hardware that is good at one specific task, while a powerful classical computer acts as the master controller. The workflow becomes a collaborative loop, a dialogue between the two different modes of computation. The classical computer, with its robust logic and massive memory, handles the overall strategy, while the quantum computer is called upon to perform the one task it is uniquely suited for: preparing and measuring a complex, entangled quantum state.

This hybrid model has found its most powerful expression in a class of algorithms known as variational algorithms. The core idea is to reframe a difficult problem not as a single, long calculation, but as an optimization task. We want to find a particular quantum state that represents the solution to our problem—for instance, the state that describes the lowest-energy configuration of a molecule. We may not know how to prepare this state directly, but we can design a "best guess" quantum circuit, known as an "ansatz," to get us close. This ansatz is not fixed; it is a flexible, tunable circuit with a set of adjustable knobs, or parameters, which are typically the rotation angles of single-qubit gates. The problem then becomes a search: what is the perfect setting for all these knobs that will make our ansatz circuit produce the desired target state?

This search is where the hybrid loop comes into play. The process begins on the classical computer, which acts as the "brains" of the operation. It chooses an initial set of parameters for the quantum circuit. These parameters are then sent to the QPU. The quantum computer, the "muscle," then does its part. It runs the shallow, parameterized ansatz circuit, preparing a quantum trial state. It then measures this state to estimate some property of interest—for example, its energy. This measurement is inherently noisy and must be repeated thousands or even millions of times to get a statistically meaningful average.

This single, classical number—the estimated energy—is then passed back to the classical computer. The classical machine now consults a powerful optimization algorithm, a piece of software that is a workhorse of classical machine learning and data science. This optimizer looks at the energy result and says, "Okay, that was our score for that set of parameters. Let's try adjusting the knobs this way and see if we can do better." It then proposes a new, slightly different set of parameters, and the whole loop begins again. The process is repeated over and over, with the classical optimizer intelligently guiding the quantum circuit, step by step, "downhill" toward the lowest possible energy. It is a quantum-assisted search, with each part of the system playing to its strengths.

The most prominent and promising of these variational methods is the Variational Quantum Eigensolver, or VQE. Its primary target is the notoriously difficult problem of quantum chemistry. Accurately calculating the ground state energy of a molecule is a problem that scales exponentially with the number of electrons, quickly overwhelming even the most powerful supercomputers. This is a task of immense practical importance, as this energy value is the key to understanding a molecule's properties, its stability, and how it will react with other molecules. It is the holy grail for designing new drugs and creating novel materials.

VQE tackles this problem head-on using the hybrid loop. The ansatz circuit is designed based on the physics of the specific molecule being studied. The classical optimizer guides the search, and the QPU prepares and measures trial quantum states that represent different electronic configurations of the molecule. The goal is to find the parameter settings that produce the state with the absolute minimum energy. VQE is a powerful idea because it is inherently noise-resilient. A small amount of noise on the QPU might lead to a slightly inaccurate energy measurement in one step, but the classical optimizer is often robust enough to find its way to the correct minimum anyway. It is an approach designed from the ground up to work on imperfect hardware.

A close cousin of VQE is the Quantum Approximate Optimization Algorithm, or QAOA. While VQE is aimed at the world of chemistry and materials science, QAOA sets its sights on the vast and challenging landscape of combinatorial optimization. These are the "needle in a haystack" problems that plague industries from logistics and finance to network design. The Traveling Salesman Problem is a classic example: given a list of cities, what is the shortest possible route that visits each city once? The number of possible routes grows astronomically with the number of cities, making a brute-force search impossible.

QAOA attacks these problems with the same variational strategy. A classical optimization loop is used to tune a shallow quantum circuit. In this case, the goal of the circuit is to prepare a quantum state that, when measured, has a high probability of collapsing to the classical bit string that represents the optimal solution to the problem. The "cost function" that the classical optimizer seeks to minimize is directly related to the problem itself—for example, the total length of a salesman's route. By iteratively preparing and measuring quantum states, the algorithm "feels out" the landscape of possible solutions, guided by the classical optimizer toward the most promising regions. Like VQE, QAOA is not guaranteed to find the perfect answer, especially on noisy hardware, but it holds the potential to find better approximate solutions than classical computers can in a reasonable amount of time.

This variational approach is also making inroads into the burgeoning field of quantum machine learning. Here, parameterized quantum circuits are being explored as new kinds of machine learning models, analogous to classical neural networks. The input data is encoded into a quantum state, the parameterized circuit processes this information, and the measurement results are used to make a prediction or classification. A classical computer then compares this prediction to the correct answer and adjusts the parameters in the quantum circuit to improve its performance. The great hope is that the exponentially large computational space of a quantum processor might allow it to "see" patterns in data that are invisible to classical models. This is a very active, and very hyped, area of research, but it fits perfectly within the NISQ paradigm of using shallow, tunable circuits controlled by a classical machine.

Of course, even with these clever, noise-resilient algorithms, the raw error rates of NISQ devices are still a major barrier. This has spurred the development of a rich toolkit of quantum error mitigation techniques. Unlike the grand, long-term project of error correction, error mitigation is a set of practical, software-based tricks for squeezing better performance out of the hardware we have today. The philosophy of mitigation is not to prevent or fix errors, but to measure their effects and then extrapolate them away from the final result.

The most intuitive of these techniques is zero-noise extrapolation. The idea is to run your quantum circuit multiple times, and with each run, you intentionally, and controllably, increase the amount of noise in the system. For example, you could make each CNOT gate slightly longer, knowing that this will increase its error rate. You then plot your results—say, the measured energy of a molecule—against the known noise level you introduced. You will get a series of points that show the answer getting worse as the noise increases. By fitting a curve to these points, you can then extrapolate backward to the y-axis, the point where the noise level is zero, to get a corrected estimate of the ideal, error-free result. It is a clever way of using the machine's own noise against itself to produce a better answer.

The NISQ era is, therefore, a period of intense and pragmatic innovation. It is defined by a set of hard constraints—noise and limited scale—and a set of clever strategies designed to work within those constraints. It is an era of hybrid algorithms, variational methods, and error mitigation. The ultimate goal is to find a "NISQ-friendly" problem, a task where the quadratic or even exponential advantage offered by a quantum approach is powerful enough to overcome the debilitating effects of noise and provide a genuine, practical advantage over the best available classical methods.

It is entirely possible that this search will prove fruitless. The effects of noise may simply be too overwhelming, the required circuit depths too great, and the quantum advantage too fragile to manifest on this generation of hardware. We may find that for all real-world problems, the cleverly optimized classical algorithms running on massive supercomputers will continue to outperform our noisy quantum processors until the day that true fault tolerance is achieved. This is the great "NISQ bet." But it is a bet that the entire field is willing to take, for the potential prize is immense. It is the chance to prove, for the first time, that quantum computers are not just a futuristic dream, but a present-day reality capable of solving problems that were, until now, beyond our reach.

CHAPTER EIGHTEEN: Quantum Cryptography: Security in a Post-Quantum World

In 1994, Peter Shor did more than just publish a clever algorithm; he started a clock. It was a slow, quiet ticking at first, audible only to a small community of mathematicians and physicists, but its rhythm has been growing steadily louder ever since. This is the doomsday clock for modern cryptography. As we saw in Chapter Ten, Shor's algorithm is a quantum recipe that can take the brutally difficult problem of factoring large numbers—the very foundation of the security that protects our digital lives—and solve it with an almost casual efficiency. The lock that secures everything from our bank accounts and government secrets to our private messages is built on the assumption that no classical computer could ever pick it in a human lifetime. Shor's algorithm is the key that, one day, a sufficiently powerful quantum computer will be able to turn.

This looming threat has created a new and urgent field of study, forcing us to imagine and prepare for a "post-quantum" world. This is a future where the cryptographic assurances we have relied upon for half a century have evaporated, rendered obsolete by a new kind of computational power. The challenge is immense, for it is not just about protecting future secrets, but also about the vulnerability of our past ones. Any encrypted data that is being harvested and stored today—sensitive corporate data, classified government communications, personal health records—could be retroactively decrypted the moment a large-scale quantum computer comes online. The clock is ticking not just for the security of tomorrow, but for the privacy of yesterday.

The race is on to build a new generation of cryptographic defenses, to re-fortify our digital civilization before the quantum battering ram arrives. This effort is advancing on two parallel fronts, two fundamentally different philosophies for achieving security in the quantum age. The first is a brilliant rearguard action, a mission to find stronger classical locks. The second is a radical new approach, a plan to fight quantum fire with quantum fire, using the very laws of physics that empower the attacker to create a provably perfect defense. This is the story of how we plan to keep our secrets safe in a world where the old rules of security no longer apply.

The first line of defense is a field known as Post-Quantum Cryptography, or PQC. The name can be slightly misleading, as it does not involve using quantum computers to perform the encryption. On the contrary, PQC is the search for new *classical* cryptographic algorithms that can be run on our existing classical computers but are believed to be secure against attacks from both classical and future quantum computers. It is, in essence, a software upgrade for the world's security infrastructure. The goal is to find a new mathematical trapdoor, one whose difficulty does not rely on problems like factoring that we know are easy for a quantum computer.

Computer scientists and mathematicians are exploring a variety of new computational problems that they believe are hard for all computers, quantum included. Instead of basing security on the difficulty of factoring, these new systems are built on different mathematical foundations. One promising area is lattice-based cryptography, which relies on the difficulty of finding the shortest path between points in a complex, high-dimensional grid, or lattice. Another is code-based cryptography, which hides messages within complex error-correcting codes. Others include hash-based signatures and multivariate cryptography. While the underlying mathematics is fiendishly complex, the guiding principle is simple: find a problem that is easy to compute in one direction (the encryption) but appears to have no hidden structure, like periodicity, that a quantum algorithm like Shor's could exploit to solve it in the other direction (the decryption).

This global search for our next cryptographic standard is not happening in a vacuum. It is being led by institutions like the U.S. National Institute of Standards and Technology (NIST), which in 2016 launched a public competition to find and standardize the most promising PQC algorithms. For years, cryptographers from around the world have been submitting their best ideas, which are then subjected to a grueling process of public scrutiny, analysis, and attack by the entire global research community. It is a cryptographic battle royale, designed to ensure that only the strongest and most resilient algorithms survive. In 2022, NIST announced its first set of winners, marking a major milestone in the transition to a quantum-resistant world. The great advantage of PQC is its practicality. It is a drop-in replacement for our current systems. Implementing it will be a massive global software and hardware update, but it does not require building any new, exotic quantum infrastructure.

While PQC is a pragmatic and essential defense, its security still rests on a familiar foundation: an assumption of computational difficulty. We *believe* these new lattice problems are hard for quantum computers, but we do not have a fundamental proof that they are. This leaves open the unsettling possibility that another brilliant mind, a future Peter Shor, could one day discover a new quantum algorithm that breaks these systems as well. This is where the second front in the security war opens, a front that offers a far more absolute, and far more "spooky," form of protection. This is the realm of true quantum cryptography.

The central idea of quantum cryptography is to use the fundamental laws of quantum mechanics itself to secure our communications. Instead of relying on the assumed difficulty of a math problem, its security is guaranteed by the very bedrock of physics. The most developed and important application of this idea is called Quantum Key Distribution, or QKD. QKD is not an encryption algorithm itself; it is a solution to the most vexing problem in all of cryptography: the secure exchange of a secret key.

For centuries, the holy grail of secret communication has been the one-time pad. It is a simple and beautiful idea. To send a secret message, you first create a completely random secret key that is the same length as the message. You then combine this key with your message (classically, using a simple XOR operation) to create the encrypted text. The recipient, who has the only other copy of the secret key, can then use it to perfectly reverse the process and reveal the original message. It has been mathematically proven that, if the key is truly random, used only once, and kept perfectly secret, the one-time pad is an unconditionally secure, unbreakable form of encryption. It is perfect.

The problem, of course, has always been the last part: keeping the key perfectly secret. How do you get the key from the sender (whom we will call Alice) to the receiver (Bob) without an eavesdropper (Eve) getting a copy? If you could meet in person to exchange the key in a locked room, you would be set. But if you have to send the key over a communication channel, how can you be sure no one is listening in? This is the key distribution problem, and it is precisely what QKD is designed to solve. QKD is a method for Alice and Bob to create and share a secret key in such a way that the laws of quantum mechanics guarantee that any attempt by Eve to intercept it will be instantly detected.

To understand how this works, we must return to the strange behavior of a single qubit, in this case, a single photon. We can encode a bit of information onto a photon using its polarization. For example, we can decide that a horizontal polarization ($\leftrightarrow$) represents a 0, and a vertical polarization ($\updownarrow$) represents a 1. This is known as the rectilinear basis. But we could also choose a different encoding scheme, the diagonal basis, where a 45-degree polarization ($\nearrow$) represents a 0, and a 135-degree polarization ($\nwarrow$) represents a 1.

The crucial quantum rule is this: you can only measure a photon's polarization perfectly if you use the correct basis. If Alice sends a vertically polarized photon (a "1" in the rectilinear basis) and Bob measures it using the rectilinear basis, he will get "1" with 100% certainty. But if Bob decides to measure that same photon using the diagonal basis, the outcome is completely random. The act of measuring in the wrong basis forces the photon to "choose" one of the diagonal states, giving him a 50% chance of getting "0" ($\nearrow$) and a 50% chance of getting "1" ($\nwarrow$). The measurement has not only yielded a random result, but it has also irretrievably altered the photon's original state. This is the observer effect, and it is Eve's worst nightmare.

The most famous QKD protocol, known as BB84 after its inventors Bennett and Brassard, harnesses this principle in an elegant four-step dance. In the first step, Alice creates a random string of classical bits she wants to turn into a key. For each bit, she also randomly chooses one of the two bases (rectilinear or diagonal) to encode it. She then sends her message to Bob one photon at a time. For instance, to send a "1," she might randomly choose the diagonal basis and send a 135-degree (↖) polarized photon. To send a "0," she might randomly choose the rectilinear basis and send a horizontally (↔) polarized photon. Bob receives this stream of single photons, completely unaware of which basis Alice used for each one.

In the second step, as each photon arrives, Bob must make a choice. For each photon, he randomly chooses to measure it in either the rectilinear or the diagonal basis. He records his choice of basis and the measurement result for every photon. At this point, Bob has a string of bits, but it is mostly garbage. For the photons where he happened to guess the same basis as Alice, his result will be correct. But for the roughly 50% of photons where he guessed the wrong basis, his result will be completely random.

The third step, often called "sifting," is where the magic starts. Alice and Bob now get on a regular, public communication channel, like a phone line or the internet. This channel does not need to be secure; Eve can listen in to this part all she wants. Over this channel, Alice and Bob simply compare the sequence of bases they used for each photon. They do not reveal the bits they sent or measured, only the basis choice. For every photon where they discover they used a different basis, they throw their corresponding bit away. For all the photons where their basis choices matched, they keep their bit. The string of bits they are left with is now the shared, secret key. In an ideal world, their keys should be identical.

This brings us to the fourth and final step: security checking. What if Eve was trying to intercept the key during the initial photon transmission? Let's say Eve intercepts one of Alice's photons on its way to Bob. To learn the bit, Eve has to measure it. But she, like Bob, has no idea which basis Alice used. She has to guess. If she guesses the correct basis, she can measure the photon, learn the bit, and re-transmit an identical photon to Bob, remaining completely invisible. But 50% of the time, she will guess the wrong basis. When this happens, her measurement will not only give her a random result, but it will also change the photon's polarization. The photon she sends on to Bob is now corrupted.

Later, during the sifting phase, this corrupted photon might be one of the ones Alice and Bob decide to keep because their bases matched. But because Eve altered it, Bob's measurement might now be different from Alice's original bit. The result is that Eve's snooping will inevitably introduce errors into Bob's version of the sifted key. To detect this, Alice and Bob take a small, randomly chosen sample of their final key and compare these bits over the public channel. If the keys are identical (or have a very low error rate, to account for imperfections in the physical hardware), they can be highly confident that no one was listening. They then discard the publicly revealed sample bits and use the rest of the key for their one-time pad. If, however, they find an error rate that is higher than expected, they know Eve was on the line. They must assume the entire key has been compromised, so they throw it away and start the entire process over from the beginning. Eve cannot gain information about the key without revealing her own presence. The security is guaranteed by the laws of physics.

This is not science fiction. QKD systems are a reality. They are commercially available today from several companies and have been deployed to secure communication links for banks, governments, and research institutions around the world. China has even launched a satellite, Micius, dedicated to performing quantum communication experiments, successfully demonstrating QKD between the satellite and ground stations separated by over a thousand kilometers. This technology provides an unparalleled level of security for data in transit.

However, QKD is not a panacea, and it comes with its own set of significant practical challenges. The first is distance. Single photons are fragile things. As they travel through a fiber optic cable, they are prone to being absorbed or scattered. After about 100 kilometers of standard fiber, the signal becomes too weak to be useful. This point-to-point distance limitation is a major hurdle for building a global quantum network. Researchers are working on two solutions: "trusted nodes," which are essentially secure repeater stations that receive a key and then re-transmit it on a new QKD link, and the far more advanced concept of a "quantum repeater," a complex device that uses quantum entanglement to extend the range of a quantum link without ever needing to trust an intermediary node.

It is also crucial to remember what QKD does and does not do. It provides a provably secure way to generate and share a secret key. It does not encrypt the actual data itself, nor does it secure data that is at rest, stored on a hard drive. Once Alice and Bob have their key, they still use classical encryption—the one-time pad—to protect their message. The security of the QKD hardware itself is also a point of vulnerability. If Eve can hack the classical computers controlling Alice's or Bob's QKD devices, she can steal the key without ever touching a photon. Securing these endpoints is just as important as securing the quantum channel.

This leaves us with a future secured by two complementary technologies. Post-Quantum Cryptography will be our workhorse, a vital software upgrade that protects the vast majority of our digital interactions and secures our stored data from future quantum attacks. It is the new, stronger deadbolt on every digital door. Quantum Key Distribution, in contrast, is the high-security armored car. It is a hardware-based solution for situations that require the absolute, highest level of proven security for communications in transit. It will be used to create ultra-secure backbones between data centers, government facilities, and financial institutions. In the coming post-quantum world, our security will no longer rest on a single wall, but on a layered defense, a clever combination of classical mathematical ingenuity and the beautiful, spooky guarantees of the quantum realm itself.

CHAPTER NINETEEN: Quantum Simulation: Modeling the Universe

In 1981, long before the first qubit was ever built, the physicist Richard Feynman stood before an audience at MIT and issued a challenge that would, in many ways, define the entire field of quantum computing. He was contemplating a profound and frustrating limitation of our classical computers. We live in a world that is, at its most fundamental level, quantum mechanical. The intricate dance of electrons in a molecule, the strange collective behavior of particles in a magnet, the very nature of matter itself—all are governed by the strange and probabilistic rules of the quantum realm. Yet, the tools we had built to understand this world, our digital computers, spoke a completely different language. They spoke the deterministic, binary language of bits. Feynman's frustration was palpable. "Nature isn't classical, dammit," he famously declared, "and if you want to make a simulation of Nature, you'd better make it quantum mechanical."

This was not merely a complaint; it was a blueprint. Feynman had identified the original "killer app" for a quantum computer. He envisioned a new kind of device, a controllable quantum system that could be used to mimic, or simulate, the behavior of another, less accessible quantum system. This idea, which predates even the concept of quantum algorithms for factoring or searching, remains one of the most promising and actively pursued applications for quantum hardware. It is a quest to build a computer that thinks in the universe's native tongue, a machine designed not just to compute with numbers, but to model reality itself at its most granular level.

The core of Feynman's argument rests on a problem of exponential scaling. Why is it so mind-bogglingly difficult for a classical computer to simulate a quantum system? The reason is that quantum systems can exist in a superposition of a vast number of states, and these states are often entangled. To accurately describe the state of even a modestly sized molecule, a classical computer must keep track of the probability amplitude for every single possible configuration of its electrons. This is a task of Sisyphean proportions.

Consider a simple molecule. Each of its electrons can have a property called "spin," which can be either "up" or "down." If we have, say, 50 interacting electrons, a classical computer trying to simulate this system would need to store and manipulate a list of 2^{50} complex numbers. This is a number in the quadrillions. The amount of memory required to simply write down the quantum state would be measured in petabytes, dwarfing the capacity of even the largest supercomputers. And with each additional electron, the problem doubles in size. It is a computational wall that grows exponentially, and no amount of classical processing power can ever hope to scale it. We are trying to describe a rich, high-dimensional symphony using only the words "loud" and "quiet."

This is where the paradigm of quantum simulation offers a brilliant and elegant solution. Instead of trying to describe the quantum state with a vast list of classical numbers, why not just build it? A quantum simulator is a machine that uses its own qubits to directly represent the components of the target system. To simulate our 50-electron molecule, we could use a quantum computer with 50 qubits. Each qubit's state could correspond to the spin of one of the electrons. The quantum computer doesn't need to store a list of nine quadrillion numbers; it simply creates a 50-qubit state that is a direct, one-to-one analogue of the molecular state itself. It is the ultimate form of "show, don't tell." The simulation tackles the exponential complexity by embodying it, becoming a tiny, controllable facsimile of the very system it is trying to understand.

This powerful idea branches into two distinct, but related, approaches. The first, and most aligned with the general-purpose vision of quantum computing, is known as digital quantum simulation. This is the gate-based approach, where we use a universal quantum computer, like the ones we have been discussing, to run a program that simulates the target system. The process is analogous to how a classical computer can simulate the weather. We don't build a miniature storm in a box; we write down the mathematical equations that govern the weather and solve them step by step on our processor.

In digital quantum simulation, the goal is to break down the continuous, smooth evolution of the target system into a series of small, discrete time steps. For each tiny slice of time, we approximate the system's natural evolution using a sequence of our standard quantum gates—Hadamards, CNOTs, and various rotations. This technique, often called "Trotterization," allows us to translate the physics of a molecule or a material into the language of a quantum circuit. By applying this sequence of gates over and over, we can watch our quantum state evolve step-by-step, effectively creating a movie of how the real-world system would behave. The great advantage of the digital approach is its universality. In principle, any quantum system can be simulated on a universal quantum computer, provided you have enough qubits and a deep enough circuit. This is the long-term vision for the field.

The second approach is known as analog quantum simulation. If the digital simulator is a universal, programmable computer, the analog simulator is more like a specialized, custom-built scale model. Instead of breaking the problem down into a sequence of gates, the idea here is to build a piece of hardware whose internal physics directly mirrors the physics of the system we want to study. We don't program the simulation; we build it.

For example, imagine we want to understand how electrons move through the crystal lattice of a new material. An analog quantum simulator for this problem might consist of an array of individual, neutral atoms, each held in place by a laser beam, forming a structure of "optical tweezers." The atoms in this "optical lattice" can be made to interact with each other in ways that are mathematically identical to how electrons interact in the real solid. By nudging these atoms and watching how they move and settle, physicists can directly observe the quantum phenomena, like the emergence of magnetism or superconductivity, that they are trying to understand.

This analog approach is less flexible than its digital cousin—a simulator built to model one material cannot easily be repurposed to model a different one—but it is often far more practical to build with today's technology. It sidesteps the need for the millions or billions of high-fidelity gates required for a deep digital simulation. Instead, it lets nature do the hard work, leveraging the natural evolution of a well-controlled quantum system to find the answer. For many researchers, these specialized analog devices represent the most promising near-term path to solving problems that are currently beyond the reach of classical simulation.

The potential applications of these techniques are vast and transformative, touching nearly every corner of modern science and technology. The most immediate and eagerly anticipated impact is in the fields of quantum chemistry and materials science, areas we will explore in greater detail in a subsequent chapter. The ability to calculate, from first principles, the precise properties of a molecule is the holy grail of drug discovery. Quantum simulators promise to allow us to screen candidate drug molecules on a quantum computer, predicting their effectiveness and side effects with an accuracy that is currently unimaginable. This could slash the time and cost of developing new medicines from years to months.

Similarly, in materials science, quantum simulation is a tool for invention. Many of the greatest technological challenges we face, from clean energy to efficient transportation, are fundamentally materials science problems. We need better catalysts to capture carbon from the atmosphere, we need more efficient materials for solar cells, we need better batteries to store renewable energy, and we dream of finding a material that can superconduct electricity at room temperature, a discovery that would revolutionize the power grid. These materials are governed by complex quantum mechanics. Quantum simulation provides a new kind of laboratory, a computational microscope that will allow us to understand these systems and, ultimately, to design new materials with the exact properties we desire.

Beyond these practical applications, quantum simulation is also poised to become a powerful tool for fundamental scientific discovery. There are realms of physics that are simply impossible to explore with terrestrial experiments. We cannot create the incomprehensible density of a neutron star in a lab, nor can we rewind the clock to observe the state of the universe moments after the Big Bang. These extreme environments are natural homes for quantum simulation. By encoding the known laws of high-energy nuclear physics or cosmology into a quantum computer, we can create small-scale, controllable models of these exotic systems. We could simulate the merger of two black holes, watch the formation of quantum fields in the early universe, or probe the mysteries of dark matter. It is a tool that allows us to conduct experiments in realms where experiments are impossible.

This brings us back to the reality of the NISQ era. While the grandest of these visions—simulating a complex protein or the heart of a neutron star—will almost certainly require large-scale, fault-tolerant quantum computers, the field of quantum simulation is widely regarded as the most promising application for the noisy, intermediate-scale machines we have today. The reason for this optimism is that for many simulation problems, you do not need a perfect, error-free answer to gain a significant advantage.

Classical simulation methods are often forced to make gross simplifications and approximations to make problems tractable. A quantum simulation, even a noisy one, starts from a more fundamentally correct physical picture. A simulation run on a NISQ device might not yield the exact ground state energy of a molecule, but it may produce an approximation that is still better than what a classical computer could achieve. This is particularly true for the hybrid, variational algorithms like VQE we encountered earlier. VQE is, at its heart, a NISQ-friendly algorithm for quantum simulation. It uses a shallow quantum circuit to prepare a trial state and leverages a classical optimizer to navigate the noisy landscape, making it a robust and pragmatic tool for the hardware we have right now.

The journey to fulfilling Feynman's vision is still in its early stages. The challenges are immense. For digital simulation, the primary hurdle is the need for much deeper circuits and higher-fidelity gates than are currently available. The "Trotter errors" that arise from approximating continuous time with discrete steps can accumulate quickly, and developing more efficient ways to translate physical problems into gate sequences is a major area of research. For analog simulation, the challenge lies in improving the degree of control and expanding the range of physical interactions that can be engineered in the lab. For both, the problem of accurately preparing the initial quantum state and efficiently reading out the final result remains a significant bottleneck.

Despite these hurdles, the progress is tangible. Every year, experimentalists are simulating slightly larger and more complex molecules. They are building analog simulators with more atoms that can model more intricate quantum phenomena. Each of these experiments is a small but crucial step, a test of our control over the quantum world and a glimpse of the computational power that lies within. Feynman's challenge was to build a machine that operates on the same principles as nature itself. We are now, for the first time in history, beginning to build such machines. We are learning to construct tiny, programmable universes in a bottle, and in doing so, we are gaining a new and profound power to understand the much larger one that surrounds us.

CHAPTER TWENTY: Quantum Machine Learning: AI on a Quantum Scale

We find ourselves living through two parallel technological revolutions, each unfolding at a breathtaking pace and each promising to reshape our world in fundamental ways. The first is the ongoing explosion in artificial intelligence, driven by the power of machine learning. From the algorithms that recommend our next movie to the systems that are learning to drive our cars, machine learning has become the engine of the modern digital economy. The second revolution, the one that is the subject of this book, is the dawn of quantum computing, a complete reimagining of the physical basis of computation itself. It is only natural to ask: what happens when these two monumental forces collide? What new possibilities emerge when we combine the learning power of AI with the computational power of the quantum realm?

This intersection is the burgeoning and exhilarating field of quantum machine learning, or QML. The very name conjures up science-fiction images of conscious, sentient quantum computers. The reality, at least for the foreseeable future, is something far more practical, yet no less profound. QML is not about creating artificial consciousness; it is about harnessing the unique principles of quantum mechanics to solve some of the most challenging problems in machine learning. It is an attempt to build a new class of algorithms that can learn from data in a way that is fundamentally different from their classical counterparts, potentially unlocking insights that have remained hidden until now.

To understand the core motivation behind QML, we must return to a central theme of this book: the immense information-carrying capacity of a quantum system. A classical computer, at its heart, processes data in a straightforward, flat space. A data point with a hundred features is simply a point in a hundred-dimensional space. While this is a powerful paradigm, it has its limits. As the number of features grows, the volume of this space explodes, making it increasingly difficult for classical algorithms to find patterns. This is the infamous "curse of dimensionality," a major hurdle in many areas of machine learning. A quantum computer, by contrast, operates in an exponentially larger and more complex arena known as Hilbert space. The state of just a hundred qubits lives in a space with 2^{100} dimensions.

This vastness is the central opportunity of QML. The core idea is to take our classical data, with all its high-dimensional complexity, and map it into this even more expansive quantum state space. By representing our data not as a string of bits, but as a rich, entangled quantum state, a quantum computer might be able to "see" the problem from a completely new vantage point. It could potentially identify correlations and structures within the data that are completely invisible in the original classical space. It is like trying to understand the relationship between cities on a globe. A classical computer might be limited to looking at a flat, distorted Mercator projection, while a quantum computer has the power to see the problem on the sphere itself, where the true relationships are immediately apparent.

The first and most critical step in this process is getting the classical data into the quantum computer in the first place. You cannot simply upload a JPEG file into a qubit. This translation is performed by a special type of quantum circuit known as a "quantum feature map." This circuit is a recipe that takes a classical data point—a vector of numbers representing, for example, the pixel values of an image or the financial metrics of a stock—and encodes it as a specific quantum state. The design of this feature map is not just a technicality; it is the art and science at the heart of many QML algorithms. A well-designed feature map can act as a powerful transformation. It can take a dataset where the different classes are hopelessly jumbled together and map them to a quantum state space where they become cleanly and easily separable. This is conceptually similar to the "kernel trick" used in classical machine learning algorithms like support vector machines, but the quantum version offers access to a potentially much richer and more powerful set of transformations.

The most active and promising area of QML research today focuses on using this principle in a hybrid quantum-classical framework, a strategy perfectly suited to the NISQ era. The quantum computer is used as a specialized co-processor, tasked with exploring the quantum feature space, while a classical computer handles the overall learning and optimization. One of the most prominent examples of this synergy is the development of quantum kernels for classical machine learning models. A support vector machine, or SVM, is a popular classical algorithm that works by finding the optimal dividing line, or hyperplane, that separates data into different categories. To do this for complex, non-linear data, it relies on a "kernel function," which is a mathematical recipe for calculating the similarity between any two data points in a high-dimensional space.

The quantum-enhanced version of this idea is wonderfully direct. Instead of calculating this kernel function on a classical computer, we outsource the job to the QPU. We take two data points, use a quantum feature map to encode each of them into a quantum state, and then use a simple quantum circuit to measure the "overlap" or similarity between these two states. This quantum-calculated similarity score is our kernel. We repeat this process for many pairs of data points, building up a "kernel matrix" that is then fed back to a completely classical SVM algorithm, which proceeds to find the best separating boundary as usual. The hope is that the quantum computer's ability to measure similarity in its vast Hilbert space will allow the classical algorithm to find better, more accurate classification boundaries than it ever could on its own.

A second major family of hybrid algorithms are the variational quantum classifiers, or VQCs. These are the machine learning cousins of the VQE and QAOA algorithms we encountered previously. VQCs are often described as a form of quantum neural network and are trained in a now-familiar hybrid loop. The process starts by encoding a data point into a quantum state using a feature map. This state is then passed through a shallow, parameterized quantum circuit, which is the quantum equivalent of a neural network layer. The parameters are a set of tunable knobs, typically the rotation angles of the gates in the circuit. After the circuit is run, one or more qubits are measured. The measurement outcome, for example, the probability of measuring a $|1\rangle$, is interpreted as the model's prediction.

This prediction is then sent back to a classical computer, which compares it to the correct, known label from the training data. The classical machine calculates the error and then calls upon a powerful classical optimization algorithm to suggest a new set of parameters for the quantum circuit, with the goal of reducing that error. This loop of proposing parameters, running on the QPU, measuring, and updating on the classical computer is repeated, sometimes for thousands of iterations, until the model learns to accurately classify the data. The quantum circuit itself is the "model," and the classical computer acts as the "trainer," slowly and intelligently tuning the quantum model until it performs its task well.

Beyond these practical, NISQ-era hybrid approaches, theorists have also identified quantum algorithms that could, in principle, offer dramatic, exponential speedups for certain core machine learning tasks. The most famous of these is the HHL algorithm, named for its creators Harrow, Hassidim, and Lloyd. The HHL algorithm is a quantum method for solving systems of linear equations, which is a fundamental mathematical operation that lies at the heart of a vast number of classical ML algorithms, from linear regression to principal component analysis. The algorithm promises an exponential speedup over its classical counterparts, a prospect that has generated enormous excitement.

However, this promise comes with a long and daunting list of caveats that are crucial to understanding the real-world prospects of QML. The HHL algorithm's speedup is only realized if the system of equations has certain specific properties (for example, the matrix describing it must be "sparse"). More importantly, it requires a large, fault-tolerant quantum computer, something we are still many years away from building. It also relies on the existence of an efficient "quantum RAM" or QRAM to load the massive classical data into a superposition, a piece of hardware whose physical feasibility is still an open question. Finally, the output of the HHL algorithm is not a classical list of numbers representing the solution; it is a quantum state that encodes the solution. Extracting the full classical answer from this state can cancel out the exponential speedup in many cases.

This brings us to the great challenges and the significant hype surrounding the field of QML. It is an area of immense theoretical promise, but it is also one where the practical hurdles are monumental. The first of these is the data loading bottleneck. Machine learning thrives on massive datasets. The very idea of "big data" is central to its success. But how do you efficiently load terabytes of classical information into a quantum computer? If loading the data takes longer than it would for a classical computer to simply solve the problem, then any quantum speedup in the processing stage is irrelevant. This is a fundamental obstacle for which there is currently no easy solution.

The second, and most immediate, challenge is noise. The variational algorithms that are the workhorses of the NISQ era are designed to be somewhat noise-resilient, but they are not immune. The noise in today's processors limits the depth of the quantum circuits we can run and the accuracy of the measurements we can obtain. As a result, almost all current QML experiments are performed on very small, "toy" datasets, often with only a handful of features. Demonstrating a genuine quantum advantage on a real-world, large-scale dataset remains an elusive goal.

Furthermore, a troubling theoretical discovery has emerged in recent years that poses a significant threat to the scalability of many variational approaches. This is the problem of "barren plateaus." Researchers have found that for many common types of parameterized quantum circuits, as the number of qubits grows, the optimization landscape becomes exponentially flat. This means that the gradients—the signals that tell the classical optimizer which direction to move in to improve the model—become vanishingly small. The optimizer is left flying blind in a vast, featureless desert, unable to find its way to the solution. Overcoming the challenge of barren plateaus is one of the most critical open research questions in the field.

Finally, the bar for demonstrating a true quantum advantage in machine learning is exceptionally high. Classical machine learning is not a static target; it is one of the most rapidly advancing fields in all of science. New algorithms, new neural network architectures, and new specialized hardware like GPUs and TPUs are constantly pushing the boundaries of what is possible. For a QML algorithm to be considered truly useful, it must outperform not just a simple textbook algorithm, but the very best, most highly optimized classical methods running on state-of-the-art hardware. This is a formidable benchmark.

The field of quantum machine learning is, therefore, a landscape of breathtaking peaks and deep valleys. The theoretical promise of harnessing the vast computational space of a quantum processor to understand data is a powerful and compelling vision. However, the path to realizing this vision is fraught with fundamental and practical challenges that are far from being solved. The most likely near-term successes will not come from quantum computers replacing all of classical machine learning. Instead, they will likely emerge from niche applications, perhaps in analyzing data that is itself quantum in origin, such as the output of a quantum simulation of a molecule. For now, QML is best viewed not as an impending tidal wave set to sweep away classical AI, but as the slow and steady development of a completely new set of tools, which, once mature, may become an indispensable part of the ever-expanding toolkit of artificial intelligence.

CHAPTER TWENTY-ONE: Quantum's Impact on Medicine and Materials

For much of our journey so far, we have been explorers in a new world of computation, learning its strange language and mapping its unfamiliar terrain. We have seen how the peculiar rules of the quantum realm can be harnessed to build powerful algorithms for tasks like factoring and searching. But now, we turn our attention from the abstract beauty of algorithms to the tangible, physical world around us. We come full circle, back to the very challenge that first inspired Richard Feynman to dream of a quantum computer: the profound difficulty of understanding and predicting the behavior of matter itself at its most fundamental level.

It is in the intricate, subatomic dance of molecules and materials that quantum mechanics reigns supreme. This is the world where the next generation of life-saving drugs will be designed and the revolutionary materials needed to solve our greatest energy and environmental challenges will be invented. Yet, this is also the world that has stubbornly resisted our best efforts at classical simulation. The exponential complexity of quantum interactions has formed a computational wall, a barrier that has forced scientists to rely on a slow, expensive, and often frustrating process of trial and error. The promise of quantum computing in these fields is not merely to speed up our current methods, but to knock down that wall entirely. It is to provide a new kind of laboratory, an *in silico* workbench where we can design the building blocks of our future, atom by atom.

The central obstacle that has stymied classical computers is a phenomenon known as the electronic structure problem. A molecule, at its heart, is a collection of atomic nuclei and a cloud of electrons that bind them together. The properties of that molecule—its shape, its stability, how it will react with other molecules—are all dictated by the precise configuration of this electron cloud. Finding this lowest-energy, or "ground state," configuration is the key to all of chemistry. The problem is that electrons are not independent, solitary particles. They are sociable, and their behavior is deeply interconnected. Each electron in the molecule is constantly interacting with every other electron, a complex and dynamic web of repulsion and attraction governed by the laws of quantum mechanics.

This interconnectedness, often called electron correlation, is the source of the exponential difficulty. A classical computer, in its attempt to solve this problem, cannot simply place electrons into orbitals one by one. It must calculate the state of the entire, vast, interconnected system at once. For a molecule with just a few dozen electrons, the number of possible configurations and interactions that must be tracked becomes astronomically large, exceeding the capacity of even the world's fastest supercomputers. To cope with this impossible task, computational chemists have developed a brilliant toolkit of approximation methods over the past several decades. Techniques like Density Functional Theory (DFT) have been remarkably successful for many systems, but they are, at their core, approximations. They rely on clever mathematical simplifications that can sometimes break down, especially for the most complex and interesting molecules where strong electron correlation effects are dominant. It is in these hard cases, where classical approximations fail, that a quantum computer can truly shine.

A quantum computer attacks the electronic structure problem not by trying to write down an impossibly long list of numbers, but by becoming the molecule itself. Using its qubits to represent the electronic orbitals, a quantum simulator can build a direct, one-to-one analogue of the molecule's quantum state. It sidesteps the exponential scaling problem by embodying it. The complex web of entanglement between its qubits can be made to directly mirror the complex web of correlation between the electrons. By preparing this analogue state and measuring its properties, the quantum computer can, in principle, calculate the molecule's ground state energy and other properties from the first principles of physics, with an accuracy that is completely out of reach for any classical machine. It is a tool designed by nature to understand nature.

Nowhere is the potential impact of this capability more profound than in the field of medicine and drug discovery. The process of bringing a new drug to market is currently one of the most expensive and time-consuming endeavors in all of science, often taking over a decade and costing billions of dollars. At its heart, this process is a grand-scale search, a quest to find a single, small molecule—the drug—that can perfectly interact with a specific, large target molecule in the body, usually a protein, to produce a therapeutic effect. This interaction is often described by a "lock and key" model: the drug molecule is the key that must fit perfectly into a specific pocket on the protein, the lock, to turn it on or off.

The strength of this fit is determined by the "binding energy" between the drug and the protein. A high binding energy means a strong, effective interaction. The ability to predict this binding energy accurately before a drug is ever synthesized in a lab would be a revolutionary breakthrough. It would allow pharmaceutical companies to computationally screen vast virtual libraries containing millions or even billions of potential drug candidates, quickly discarding the duds and focusing their expensive laboratory efforts only on the most promising contenders. This is precisely where classical methods struggle. The binding energy is determined by subtle quantum mechanical interactions at the interface between the two molecules, an area often rife with the strong correlation effects that trip up classical approximation methods.

Quantum simulation offers a path to calculating these binding energies with the precision needed to make reliable predictions. A quantum computer could model the active site of the target protein and then simulate the introduction of a candidate drug molecule, calculating the change in the system's energy from first principles. This would transform drug discovery from a process of painstaking, physical trial and error into a targeted, efficient, *in silico* design process. It would be like having a perfect, atomic-resolution microscope that could not only see the lock, but could test millions of virtual keys in a matter of hours.

The ambition extends far beyond simply finding better keys for existing locks. The same principles could be applied to protein design, allowing us to create entirely new proteins and enzymes with novel functions. Enzymes are the master catalysts of biology, and designing artificial enzymes that can perform specific tasks is a major goal of synthetic biology. A quantum computer could help us understand the quantum mechanical heart of catalysis, the fleeting transition states that determine an enzyme's efficiency, allowing us to engineer new biological machines for everything from breaking down environmental pollutants to targeted cancer therapies.

This vision also ties into the long-held dream of personalized medicine. We are all genetically unique, which means our proteins are subtly different. A drug that is highly effective for one person may be less so for another, or may cause debilitating side effects. In the future, it is conceivable that we could sequence a patient's genome, identify the specific structure of their version of a target protein, and then use a quantum computer to design or select a drug that is perfectly tailored to their individual biology. It is a future where medicine is no longer a one-size-fits-all proposition, but a precisely targeted intervention designed for the individual.

Just as the future of medicine is written in the language of molecules, the future of our technological civilization is written in the language of materials. Our ability to tackle the world's most pressing challenges, from climate change and clean energy to sustainable manufacturing and next-generation transportation, is fundamentally limited by the properties of the materials we have at our disposal. We need better materials to build more efficient batteries, to harvest solar energy more effectively, and to create the powerful technologies of the future. The design of these new materials is, once again, a quantum mechanical problem of immense complexity.

Consider the urgent search for better catalysts. A catalyst is a substance that speeds up a chemical reaction without being consumed in the process. Catalysts are the unsung heroes of the modern industrial world, underpinning an estimated 35% of global

GDP. They are essential for producing everything from plastics and fuels to the fertilizers that feed the world. The famous Haber-Bosch process, for example, uses an iron-based catalyst to pull nitrogen from the air to create ammonia for fertilizer, a discovery credited with sustaining a significant fraction of the global population. However, this process is incredibly energy-intensive, consuming over 1% of the world's entire energy supply.

Nature, in contrast, has its own version of this process, carried out by an enzyme called nitrogenase, which performs the same nitrogen fixation at room temperature and pressure. The secret lies in the enzyme's complex, metal-containing active site, a quantum system so intricate that it has defied our best attempts at classical simulation. A quantum computer could, for the first time, allow us to unravel the precise quantum mechanism of nitrogenase. With this knowledge, we could hope to design a new generation of industrial catalysts that mimic nature's efficiency, drastically reducing the energy footprint of agriculture and other chemical industries. A similar logic applies to the challenge of carbon capture, where quantum simulations could help us design new materials that can selectively and efficiently bind to CO_2 molecules, pulling them directly from the atmosphere.

The transition to a clean energy economy is another area where quantum simulation could be a game-changer. The performance of a battery is determined by the complex electrochemistry that occurs at the interface between its electrode and its electrolyte. A quantum computer could help us design new battery chemistries with higher energy densities, faster charging times, and longer lifespans, breaking through the current bottlenecks that limit the range of electric vehicles and our ability to store energy from intermittent renewable sources like solar and wind. Likewise, the efficiency of a solar cell is determined by the quantum process of converting a photon of light into an excited electron. By simulating this process in novel semiconductor materials, we could design photovoltaic devices that waste less energy as heat and capture a much larger fraction of the solar spectrum.

Perhaps the most legendary and transformative prize in all of materials science is the discovery of a room-temperature superconductor. Superconductors are materials that can conduct electricity with absolutely zero resistance, meaning no energy is lost as heat. They are a perfect, lossless electrical wire. The problem is that all known superconductors only work at extremely cold, cryogenic temperatures, making them far too expensive and impractical for widespread use. A material that could superconduct at room temperature would be one of the most significant inventions in human history. It would enable a perfectly efficient power grid, saving enormous amounts of energy. It would allow for the creation of incredibly powerful magnets for everything from maglev trains and medical MRI machines to fusion energy reactors.

The physics behind the current generation of high-temperature superconductors is one of the great unsolved mysteries of modern science, a problem deeply rooted in the bizarre collective quantum behavior of many interacting electrons. It is a problem that seems tailor-made for a quantum simulator. By building and studying controllable quantum models that capture the essential physics of these materials, researchers hope to finally crack the code of high-temperature superconductivity. This understanding would not just solve a long-standing scientific puzzle; it would provide the theoretical blueprint needed to guide the search for, and perhaps even design from scratch, the holy grail of a room-temperature superconductor.

It is crucial, of course, to temper these spectacular long-term visions with a dose of near-term reality. The applications we have just discussed—designing a complex new drug or discovering a room-temperature superconductor—will almost certainly require large-scale, fault-tolerant quantum computers that are still many years, and perhaps decades, away. The path to this future is being paved today by the noisy, intermediate-scale quantum (NISQ) devices that are the focus of our current era. Scientists are not yet simulating blockbuster drugs on these machines. Instead, they are taking the vital first steps, using algorithms like the Variational

Quantum Eigensolver (VQE) to tackle the electronic structure of very small, simple molecules.

These early experiments, simulating molecules like lithium hydride (LiH) or water (H2O), are the essential proving grounds. They are the "hello, world" programs of quantum chemistry. While the answers they produce can still be easily calculated by a classical laptop, they are invaluable for benchmarking the performance of our quantum hardware, for refining our quantum algorithms, and for developing the complex software that translates a chemistry problem into a sequence of pulses sent to a QPU. Each of these small-scale simulations is a crucial test flight, providing the data and the experience needed to build the more powerful machines of the future.

The excitement is not just confined to academic laboratories. A new ecosystem is rapidly forming at the intersection of quantum computing and these traditional scientific industries. Major pharmaceutical, chemical, and manufacturing companies are now investing heavily in the field. They are building internal quantum research teams, partnering with quantum hardware startups, and running their own small-scale experiments on cloud-based quantum platforms. They are not expecting a quantum-designed product to hit the market next year. Rather, they are making a strategic investment in the future. They are learning the new tools, identifying the most promising problems within their own research and development pipelines, and positioning themselves to be "quantum ready" for the moment when the hardware finally crosses the threshold of quantum advantage. The journey will be a long one, but the first steps have been taken on a road that promises to fundamentally reshape our ability to understand and engineer the physical world.

CHAPTER TWENTY-TWO: The Quantum Economy: Industries of the Future

For the majority of this book, we have treated the quantum computer as a subject of scientific inquiry, a magnificent and complex machine born from the strange laws of physics. We have dissected its components, from the qubit to the quantum gate, and marveled at the elegant logic of its algorithms. But as these machines slowly begin to crawl out of the pristine, shielded environments of the research laboratory and onto the cloud, they cease to be solely a scientific curiosity. They become a technology. And like every transformative technology before it, from the steam engine to the microchip, it is poised to become the foundation of a new economy, the engine for industries that we are only just beginning to imagine.

The conversation is shifting. The question is no longer just "How does it work?" but "What is it worth?". The pursuit of a functional quantum computer has evolved from a quiet, academic marathon into a full-blown global race, with nations, corporations, and investors pouring billions of dollars into the field. This influx of capital and strategic interest is forging a new and complex ecosystem, a global supply chain of innovation dedicated to building and commercializing the quantum future. This is the quantum economy, and its foundations are being laid today.

At the heart of this new economy are the builders, the companies engaged in the Herculean task of constructing the quantum processors themselves. This is a landscape of both giants and pioneers. On one side are the titans of the classical computing world—companies like Google, IBM, and Microsoft—who are leveraging their immense resources, deep expertise in fabrication, and global cloud infrastructure to build their own superconducting and topological quantum processors. They are building what are known as "full-stack" systems, controlling every layer of the technology from the physical qubits at the bottom of a refrigerator to the software that users interact with at the top.

Competing alongside these giants is a vibrant and rapidly growing ecosystem of startups, each pursuing a unique approach to building a qubit. Companies like IonQ and Quantinuum are championing the trapped-ion platform, betting on its high fidelity and long coherence times. Others, like Rigetti Computing, are iterating on superconducting designs, while startups like PsiQuantum and Xanadu are pursuing the radical and ambitious path of photonics. These companies are not just competing on technical merit; they are pioneering new business models. The days of needing a multi-billion-dollar budget and a state-of-the-art physics lab to access a quantum computer are over. The dominant model for this new industry is quantum computing as a service (QCaaS). Through the cloud, anyone with an internet connection and a credit card can now write a quantum program and run it on some of the most advanced hardware in the world.

This democratization of access, powered by platforms like IBM Quantum, Amazon Braket, and Microsoft Azure Quantum, has been the single most important catalyst for the growth of the quantum economy. It has allowed a second, crucial layer of the ecosystem to flourish: the quantum software industry. A quantum computer without software is just an incredibly cold and expensive piece of scientific art. A new generation of companies is emerging to build the essential tools, compilers, and operating systems needed to bridge the enormous gap between a high-level problem and the low-level microwave pulses that manipulate qubits. These companies are building the "middleware" of the quantum age, creating software that can take a quantum circuit designed by a user and intelligently compile it to run as efficiently as possible on a specific company's noisy hardware.

This software layer is also where the application specialists live. Startups are forming to focus on building quantum solutions for specific industries. Companies like Zapata Computing and QC Ware are not building the computers themselves, but are instead focused on designing algorithms and software platforms tailored for quantum chemistry, financial modeling, or machine learning. They are the expert consultants of the NISQ era, helping large enterprise clients understand how and when this nascent technology might provide a genuine business advantage. This layered structure of hardware, cloud platforms, middleware, and application software is the signature of a maturing technological sector.

This entire private-sector ecosystem is being fueled and, in many cases, directed by a third major player: national governments. The development of a large-scale, fault-tolerant quantum computer is now widely seen as a matter of strategic national importance, akin to the development of the atomic bomb or the space race of the twentieth century. The country that first develops a machine capable of breaking modern encryption will hold an unprecedented intelligence advantage, while the one that masters quantum simulation for materials design will hold the keys to the next generation of manufacturing, energy, and defense technologies.

In response, nations around the world have launched massive, publicly funded initiatives. The United States has its National Quantum Initiative Act, a multi-billion-dollar effort to coordinate research across government labs, universities, and industry. The European Union has its Quantum Flagship program, and China has reportedly invested sums that may dwarf all others in its own national laboratories and strategic programs. This government investment is not just about funding basic research; it is about building a domestic quantum workforce, securing supply chains for critical components like dilution refrigerators and high-frequency electronics, and fostering a robust private-sector ecosystem that can translate scientific breakthroughs into economic and strategic leadership.

The final, and perhaps most important, piece of this new economy is the end user. The ultimate value of a quantum computer will not be determined by physicists, but by the chemists, financial analysts, and logistics managers who will use it to solve their most challenging problems. Large, forward-thinking corporations across a range of key industries are now beginning to engage with the technology, a process often described as becoming "quantum ready." They are not expecting to deploy a quantum solution to their production lines next year. Instead, they are making strategic investments to build internal expertise and explore potential use cases.

These companies are forming small, specialized quantum teams, hiring the first generation of quantum algorithm developers, and partnering with both hardware and software providers to run proof-of-concept experiments. A pharmaceutical company might task its team with exploring how the VQE algorithm could be applied to a specific class of drug molecules. An automotive manufacturer might investigate whether the QAOA algorithm could find a better way to optimize the paint-shop schedule in one of its factories. These early projects are about learning. They are about understanding the limitations of today's noisy hardware, benchmarking its performance against classical methods, and identifying the specific, high-value problems within their own business where a future quantum advantage might first emerge.

The financial services industry has been one of the earliest and most aggressive adopters of this quantum-ready approach. The potential payoffs are simply too large to ignore. While much attention is given to portfolio optimization—a classic NP-hard problem—the more immediate interest may lie in the complex world of risk modeling and derivatives pricing. Financial institutions rely on computationally intensive methods, most famously the Monte Carlo simulation, to model the behavior of markets and price complex financial instruments. A Monte Carlo simulation is essentially a game of sophisticated dart-throwing, where a computer runs millions or even billions of random simulations of the future to build up a statistical picture of potential outcomes. It has been shown that a quantum algorithm known as Quantum Amplitude Estimation could provide a quadratic speedup for these simulations, allowing banks to perform risk calculations faster and more accurately. This could lead to better pricing, more efficient capital allocation, and a more stable financial system.

In the worlds of automotive and aerospace manufacturing, the economic drivers are centered on efficiency and innovation. Modern manufacturing is a symphony of optimization problems.

Quantum computers, running algorithms like QAOA, are being explored as a potential tool to untangle these complex logistical puzzles. This could involve optimizing the global supply chain that brings tens of thousands of parts to a factory at just the right time, or choreographing the movements of robots on the factory floor to maximize throughput and minimize downtime. Beyond the factory, quantum computers offer the promise of fundamentally redesigning the products themselves. By using quantum simulation to design new, lightweight alloys and composite materials, manufacturers could build more fuel-efficient cars and airplanes, a direct and significant economic benefit in an energy-conscious world.

The energy and chemical sectors are similarly poised for disruption. As we explored in the previous chapter, the ability to design new catalysts from first principles could have a staggering economic impact. A catalyst that could reduce the energy requirements of the Haber-Bosch process by even a few percent would translate into billions of dollars in energy savings and a significant reduction in global carbon emissions. The economic value is not just in improving existing processes, but in enabling entirely new ones. Quantum simulation could be the key to designing the materials needed for economically viable carbon capture technologies, a breakthrough that would create a multi-trillion-dollar industry dedicated to climate change mitigation. The same logic applies to battery technology. A quantum-designed battery with double the energy density of current lithium-ion technology would not just improve our phones and laptops; it would fundamentally reshape the economics of electric transportation and renewable energy storage, accelerating the global transition away from fossil fuels.

This emerging quantum economy will require a new kind of workforce, creating a demand for skills that barely existed a decade ago. The most obvious need is for the quantum specialists themselves: the experimental physicists and electrical engineers who design and build the hardware, and the theoretical computer scientists and algorithm developers who write the software. These are the architects and builders of the new machines. However, building a thriving economy requires more than just specialists. The most critical, and currently rarest, talent is the "quantum translator." This is an individual who is a deep expert in a specific industry domain—a computational chemist, a quantitative financial analyst, a machine learning engineer—but who also possesses a strong working knowledge of quantum computing.

These translators are the essential bridge between the two worlds. They are the ones who can look at a business problem, like valuing a complex derivative, and understand how to reformulate it in a way that is amenable to a quantum algorithm. They can identify the specific, high-value challenges within their own industries where quantum methods are most likely to succeed, and they can work with the quantum specialists to design and implement meaningful experiments. Cultivating this new generation of bilingual experts is one of the greatest challenges and opportunities for universities and corporate training programs. The growth of the quantum economy will be directly limited by the pipeline of talent that can fill these crucial, interdisciplinary roles.

The financial underpinning of this entire ecosystem is a wave of both public and private investment. Venture capital firms are now placing significant bets on the sector, funding a new generation of startups in a high-risk, high-reward gamble. The investment horizons are necessarily long. Unlike a mobile app startup that might find a market in months, the path to profitability for a quantum hardware company is a decade-long marathon of deep technological development. This has led to concerns about a potential "quantum winter," a period where a slowdown in progress could lead to a contraction in funding if the near-term hype outpaces the reality of the hardware.

For now, however, the momentum is strong. The combined force of government strategic funding, venture capital investment, and the research and development budgets of large corporations is creating a powerful engine of innovation. The race is on, not just to build a single, powerful quantum computer, but to build the entire economic and industrial ecosystem that will surround it. This is a story of hardware manufacturers, cloud providers, software developers, and enterprise end-users all learning to work together. It is a story of new jobs being created and old industries being reimagined. The quantum economy is still in its infancy, a collection of promising technologies and ambitious roadmaps. But the first green shoots are visible, and they are the precursors to a technological and economic transformation that will define the century to come.

CHAPTER TWENTY-THREE: The Ethical Landscape of the Quantum Frontier

Every great technological leap forward has been a step into the unknown, a journey that has redrawn not only the map of what is possible, but also the boundaries of what is right and wrong. The steam engine brought with it immense industrial power, but also new forms of labor exploitation and societal upheaval. The digital revolution connected the globe, but also created unprecedented challenges to privacy and new vectors for misinformation. Now, as we stand at the threshold of the quantum age, we find ourselves peering into another uncharted territory, one that promises transformations just as profound and presents ethical questions just as complex. The development of quantum computing is more than just a scientific and engineering challenge; it is a call to navigate a new and bewildering ethical landscape, to consider the societal implications of this new power before it has fully arrived.

The most immediate and starkest of these ethical dilemmas stems from the technology's most famous application: its ability to break modern cryptography. As we have discussed, Peter Shor's algorithm represents a future existential threat to the encryption that underpins the security of our digital world. This is not merely a technical problem; it is a profound ethical one. The first and most pressing concern is the retroactive nature of this threat. The issue is not just about protecting future communications, but about the secrets of the past. It is widely assumed that intelligence agencies and other sophisticated actors around the world are currently engaged in a massive effort to "store now, decrypt later." They are harvesting and archiving vast quantities of encrypted data—government communications, corporate intellectual property, personal messages—under the assumption that one day they will possess a quantum computer capable of decrypting it all.

This creates a ticking time bomb for privacy and security. What is the ethical responsibility of governments and corporations to protect this legacy data? Is it sufficient to simply transition to new, post-quantum cryptographic standards for future communications, or is there a duty to protect the secrets of the past that are currently vulnerable? The very existence of this impending cryptographic break raises difficult questions about the balance between national security and individual privacy. A nation that secretly develops a large-scale quantum computer first would possess an almost unimaginable intelligence advantage, a master key to the digital secrets of its adversaries, its allies, and its own citizens. This potential for a "cryptanalytic asymmetry" could destabilize the geopolitical landscape, creating a new kind of arms race where the weapons are computational rather than kinetic. It forces us to confront the dual-use nature of this technology: the same machine that could design a new life-saving drug could also be used to dismantle the foundations of global security.

Beyond the high-stakes world of espionage and geopolitics, the advent of quantum computing promises to create significant economic and social disruption. Like previous industrial revolutions, the quantum revolution will create new industries and new forms of wealth, but it will also inevitably render old skills and old industries obsolete. The sectors poised to benefit most directly—finance, pharmaceuticals, advanced materials, and artificial intelligence—are already highly sophisticated and capital-intensive. This raises the critical question of whether quantum computing will act as a great equalizer or as a great amplifier of existing inequalities. Will the immense power of quantum optimization and simulation be concentrated in the hands of a few large corporations and wealthy nations, further widening the gap between the haves and the have-nots?

This leads to the concept of a "quantum divide," a future where access to the benefits of this transformative technology is not evenly distributed. Will a farmer in a developing nation ever see the benefits of a quantum-designed fertilizer if the intellectual property is locked away by a multinational corporation? Will a patient in a low-income country have access to a drug designed with a quantum computer if its price is astronomically high? The ethical challenge is to consider models for democratizing access to this technology, ensuring that its benefits are shared broadly across society. This extends to the workforce as well. While quantum computing will create a new class of high-skilled jobs, it may also automate and displace workers in fields like logistics, finance, and chemical engineering. Societies will have an ethical obligation to manage this transition, investing in education and social safety nets to ensure that the march of technological progress does not leave a large segment of the population behind.

The potential for misuse also extends into the very applications that make the technology so exciting. Quantum machine learning, for instance, holds the promise of creating more powerful artificial intelligence models. This immediately inherits all the ethical challenges of classical AI and potentially amplifies them. If a quantum model is used to make decisions about parole, loan applications, or medical diagnoses, how can we ensure that it is fair and unbiased? The "black box" problem, where we cannot fully understand the reasoning behind an AI's decision, could become even more pronounced with quantum models that operate in an exponentially vast and counter-intuitive computational space. Ensuring the transparency, accountability, and fairness of these future AI systems is a challenge that must be addressed from the outset.

Similarly, the power of quantum simulation, while a boon for medicine and materials science, is not inherently benevolent. The same capability that allows a scientist to design a more effective catalyst for clean energy could also be used by a rogue state or a terrorist organization to design a more deadly chemical weapon or a more virulent biological agent. The ability to model complex molecular interactions from first principles is a tool of immense power, and like all such tools, it can be wielded for both creation and destruction. This places a heavy ethical responsibility on the scientific community to establish norms, standards, and oversight mechanisms to guard against the malicious use of these powerful new simulation capabilities. The same ethical calculus applies to quantum optimization. While it could be used to create a more efficient global food distribution network, it could also be used to design a more ruthlessly efficient system of mass surveillance or to create high-frequency trading algorithms that could destabilize global financial markets for private gain.

This brings us to the crucial question of governance and control. Who gets to decide how this powerful technology is developed and deployed? In these early days, the field is a dynamic mix of academic research labs, private startups, and massive corporate projects, all heavily funded by national governments. This creates a complex web of interests and incentives. Should the development of a technology with such profound societal implications be left primarily to the forces of the market, or is there a need for stronger national and international governance? The challenge is to find a balance. Overly restrictive regulation could stifle the very innovation needed to solve some of the world's most pressing problems. An absence of regulation, on the other hand, could lead to a future where the technology is deployed irresponsibly, with little regard for its ethical consequences.

These are not questions for a distant future; the conversations are happening now. International standards bodies are working on post-quantum cryptography. Research institutions are beginning to establish ethics committees for quantum technologies. The very fact that these discussions are taking place while the technology is still in its infancy is a sign of a growing maturity in how we approach technological revolutions. There is an increasing recognition that ethical considerations cannot be an afterthought, bolted on after the technology is already mature. Instead, they must be woven into the very fabric of the research and development process. This might involve creating a code of conduct for quantum researchers, embedding ethicists within technology development teams, and fostering a broad public dialogue about the kind of quantum future we want to build.

Even the physical reality of building these machines has an ethical dimension. As currently designed, many of the leading quantum computers are enormously power-hungry. The dilution refrigerators required to cool superconducting qubits to near absolute zero are magnificent feats of engineering, but they consume a significant amount of electrical energy. As we imagine data centers filled with thousands of these machines, we must consider their environmental footprint. This presents a complex ethical trade-off. Is the energy cost of running these machines justified by the potential for them to solve our most urgent environmental challenges? The answer will likely depend on our ability to design more energy-efficient quantum hardware and to ensure that the problems we choose to solve are worthy of the cost.

The ethical landscape of the quantum frontier is vast and, in many places, still shrouded in fog. The questions are far easier to pose than to answer. They touch upon issues of international security, economic justice, individual liberty, and the very nature of responsible innovation. There are no simple, one-size-fits-all solutions. Navigating this terrain will require a sustained and collaborative effort from a wide range of stakeholders—scientists, engineers, policymakers, ethicists, social scientists, and an informed public. The challenge is not to fear the future or to halt progress, but to approach this new frontier with a sense of humility, foresight, and a deep commitment to ensuring that this extraordinary new power is ultimately used to benefit all of humanity. The work of building a quantum computer is not just about manipulating atoms; it is about choosing the kind of world we wish to create with them.

CHAPTER TWENTY-FOUR: Your Path into Quantum: How to Get Involved

Our journey through the quantum frontier is nearing its end. We began with the strange and counter-intuitive nature of the quantum realm, met the versatile qubit, and saw how the principles of superposition and entanglement could be woven into powerful new algorithms. We have peered under the hood at the magnificent and complex hardware being built to tame these principles, confronted the immense challenge of noise, and explored the grand vision of quantum error correction. We have surveyed the applications poised to reshape medicine and materials, the emergence of a new quantum economy, and the profound ethical questions that this new power demands we ask. After this long expedition into the world of tomorrow, a single, practical question remains: What now?

You have absorbed the concepts, understood the promise, and appreciated the challenges. The natural next step is to move from being a passenger on this tour to a participant in the expedition. You may be thinking that the barrier to entry is impossibly high, that the next chapter in this story is only open to those with a Ph.D. in theoretical physics and a whiteboard filled with inscrutable equations. This is, perhaps, the single greatest misconception about the field today. The quantum revolution will not be built by physicists alone. The gates to this new world are surprisingly open, and there is a clear and accessible path for anyone with a curious mind and a willingness to learn, regardless of their background. This chapter is your roadmap. It is a practical guide to transforming your curiosity into genuine engagement, your interest into tangible skills.

The first step on any new path is to discard unnecessary baggage, and for quantum computing, the heaviest piece of luggage is the myth of the lone genius. The quantum ecosystem that is rapidly taking shape is a rich and diverse one, with a pressing need for a wide array of talents. Yes, it needs experimental physicists to build the hardware and theoretical physicists to dream up new algorithms. But just as urgently, it needs computer scientists and software engineers to build the compilers, operating systems, and cloud platforms that make these machines usable. It needs electrical and mechanical engineers to design the control electronics and the cryogenic systems. It needs chemists and materials scientists who can frame their domain-specific problems in the language of quantum mechanics.

The demand extends even further. Financial analysts who understand quantum optimization will be invaluable. Machine learning experts who can navigate the world of quantum kernels will be pioneers. The industry also needs skilled project managers who can guide complex, multi-disciplinary teams, technical writers who can create clear documentation, and educators who can train the next generation of the quantum workforce. The unifying requirement is not a specific degree, but a foundational understanding of the principles and a "bilingual" ability to speak both the language of a specific application domain and the emerging language of quantum computation. The most valuable players in the coming quantum economy will be these translators, the ones who can bridge the gap between the problems of today and the solutions of tomorrow.

With this broader perspective in mind, the journey begins with assembling a foundational toolkit of knowledge. While you do not need to become an expert in all these areas, a working familiarity with a few key subjects will make your path dramatically smoother. The single most important of these is linear algebra. If quantum computing has a native language, this is it. The state of a qubit is a vector. A quantum gate is a matrix. A multi-qubit system is described by a tensor product. You do not need to master the most abstract corners of the subject, but a solid, intuitive grasp of vectors, matrices, eigenvalues, and eigenvectors is non-negotiable. It is the mathematical framework upon which the entire edifice of quantum mechanics is built.

Alongside linear algebra, a basic understanding of probability is essential. As we have seen, the outcome of a quantum measurement is fundamentally probabilistic. Being comfortable with concepts like probability distributions and expectation values will demystify the process of interpreting the results of a quantum computation. A conceptual grasp of complex numbers is also vital, as they are the mathematical key to understanding the crucial property of phase, which drives quantum interference.

Finally, for those aspiring to work on the software side of the field, a solid foundation in classical computer science is indispensable. Understanding algorithms, data structures, and particularly computational complexity theory is what allows you to appreciate *why* a quantum algorithm is powerful. The context for Shor's exponential speedup or Grover's quadratic speedup comes from understanding the classical complexity classes like P and NP. And, of course, proficiency in a programming language is a must. The lingua franca of the quantum software world today is, overwhelmingly, Python.

Armed with this foundational knowledge, the most exciting part of the journey can begin: getting your hands on a real quantum computer. A decade ago, this would have been an impossible dream. Today, it is a reality available to anyone with an internet connection, thanks to the rise of cloud-based quantum computing platforms. These services have transformed quantum computing from a cloistered academic pursuit into an open, global experiment.

The most established and accessible of these is IBM Quantum. For years, IBM has provided free public access to a fleet of its real, superconducting quantum processors. The platform features two remarkable tools for beginners. The first is the Quantum Composer, a beautiful, web-based graphical user interface that allows you to build quantum circuits by simply dragging and dropping gates onto qubit wires. It is a quantum playground, a place to build intuition by visually constructing circuits and seeing the results in real-time. The second tool is Qiskit, a comprehensive, open-source software development kit (SDK) based in Python. Qiskit is the professional's tool, a powerful library that allows you to programmatically define, compile, and run complex quantum algorithms on both simulators and IBM's state-of-the-art hardware.

Another major player in this space is Amazon Braket. Braket's defining philosophy is to be a "hardware-agnostic" platform. Instead of tying you to one type of quantum computer, it acts as a single gateway to a diverse range of machines from different providers. Through the Braket service, you can run your quantum circuit on superconducting processors from Rigetti, on trapped-ion machines from IonQ, or on photonic devices from Xanadu. This provides an unparalleled opportunity to learn about the different hardware platforms and to compare their performance on a specific problem.

Microsoft's contribution is Azure Quantum, a similarly open ecosystem that integrates a variety of hardware and software solutions into its broader Azure cloud platform. It offers access to machines from several providers and is deeply integrated with Microsoft's own Quantum Development Kit and the Q# programming language, a high-level language designed specifically for expressing quantum algorithms.

These platforms allow you to start with simulators, which are classical programs that calculate how an ideal, noise-free quantum computer would behave. Simulators are your best friend when you are learning. They are fast, they are perfect, and they allow you to inspect the full quantum state of your system at any point in the computation, a feat that is impossible on real hardware. Once you have designed and debugged your circuit on a simulator, you can then take the exhilarating step of sending it to a real QPU. This is the moment you will confront the messy reality of the NISQ era. You will see the effects of noise in your results, the perfect 50/50 split of a Bell state becoming a noisy 48/52. This is not a failure; it is your first real physics experiment.

Let's imagine what your very first quantum program might look like. Using Python and IBM's Qiskit, the process is remarkably straightforward. First, you would import the necessary components from the library. Then you would create a quantum circuit, specifying that you want two qubits and two classical bits to store the measurement results. The code would look something like this:

```
from qiskit import QuantumCircuit,
transpile, execute

from qiskit_aer import AerSimulator
```

```
# Create a quantum circuit with 2 qubits and
2 classical bits

qc = QuantumCircuit(2, 2)
```

Next, you would add the gates to create our familiar entangled Bell state. You apply a Hadamard gate to the first qubit to create superposition, and then a CNOT gate with the first qubit as the control and the second as the target to create entanglement.

```
# Add a Hadamard gate on qubit 0

qc.h(0)
```

```
# Add a CNOT gate with control qubit 0 and
target qubit 1

qc.cx(0, 1)
```

With the quantum part of the logic complete, you need to measure the qubits to extract a classical result. You would add measurement operations that map the state of the quantum bits to the classical bits.

```
# Map the quantum measurement to the
classical bits

qc.measure(,)
```

Finally, you choose your backend—in this case, a perfect classical simulator—and run the experiment. You would typically run the circuit many times (called "shots") to build up statistics.

```
# Choose the simulator backend

simulator = AerSimulator()


# Transpile the circuit for the backend

compiled_circuit = transpile(qc, simulator)


# Execute the circuit on the simulator

job = simulator.run(compiled_circuit,
shots=1024)


# Grab the results

result = job.result()
```

```
counts = result.get_counts(qc)

print("\nTotal counts are:", counts)
```

The output of this program would be a dictionary showing the number of times each outcome was measured. In a perfect simulation, you would see something like `{'00': 512, '11': 512}`, with small variations due to the randomness of sampling. In just a few lines of code, you have successfully created and measured one of the most foundational states in all of quantum mechanics. Taking the next step and running this same code on a real hardware backend is often as simple as changing a single line of code that specifies the machine's name.

This hands-on experience is the fastest way to build real intuition. To supplement it, a wealth of educational resources has sprung up to guide you on your journey. Online learning platforms like Coursera and edX host numerous introductory courses from universities and companies. IBM's Qiskit Global Summer School is a famous, intensive two-week program that is offered online, and its lectures are a fantastic resource. The free, open-source Qiskit textbook is a comprehensive and interactive guide that beautifully integrates explanations with runnable code examples.

As you progress, you will want to connect with the broader community. The quantum world is a vibrant and surprisingly collaborative one. Online forums like the Quantum Computing Stack Exchange and the subreddit r/QuantumComputing are active places to ask questions and learn from others. Following the blogs and social media accounts of the major research groups and companies will keep you up to date with the latest breakthroughs. For a deeper, more academic dive, the website arXiv.org is the open-access preprint server where almost all new scientific papers in the field first appear.

An even more powerful way to learn and connect is to participate in events. Quantum hackathons and challenges, often run by the major cloud providers, are incredible opportunities for intensive, project-based learning. They allow you to team up with other learners and mentors to tackle a real problem over a weekend. For those more academically inclined, numerous quantum summer schools offer deep dives into specific topics. And for software developers, one of the most rewarding ways to get involved is to contribute to an open-source quantum software project. Libraries like Qiskit, Google's Cirq, or the QML-focused PennyLane are all built by a global community of contributors. Making a contribution, whether it is fixing a bug, improving documentation, or adding a new feature, is a direct way to build your skills, create a public portfolio of your work, and interact with the core developers in the field.

As you build your knowledge and experience, a landscape of potential career paths will begin to come into focus. For those with a deep passion for the underlying science and a desire for advanced degrees, the traditional path of a researcher in either academia or a corporate research lab remains central to pushing the boundaries of the field. But the fastest-growing area of employment is for quantum software engineers. These are the individuals who build the tools, compilers, and applications that run on the quantum computers. A strong background in computer science and proficiency in Python, combined with a solid understanding of quantum algorithms, makes for an incredibly sought-after skill set.

On the hardware side, the demand for experimental physicists and engineers continues to grow. These are the people who are in the lab, building the machines, designing the chips, and fighting the daily battle against decoherence. The role of the "quantum translator" or application scientist is also becoming increasingly critical. These are the domain experts—the chemists, the financiers, the machine learning engineers—who can identify the right problems and map them onto the quantum hardware. As the industry matures, it is also creating a need for all the supporting roles that define a healthy technological ecosystem, from product managers and technical writers to sales engineers and developer advocates.

The path into the quantum world is not a single, narrow track, but a broad, branching network of trails. It is a field defined not by its gatekeepers, but by its open gates. The resources are available, the community is welcoming, and the hardware is, for the first time in history, accessible to all. The journey requires dedication, and the learning curve can be steep, but it is a climb that is well worth the effort. Every new concept you master, every line of quantum code you write, and every noisy result you get back from a real QPU is a step onto a new frontier. You are joining a global community of pioneers at the very beginning of a new technological age, and the most exciting discoveries are the ones that have not yet been made.

CHAPTER TWENTY-FIVE: The Next Frontier: Peering into the Quantum Future

Our exploration of the quantum world has taken us from the baffling mystery of a single electron passing through two slits at once to the intricate, global effort to build a new kind of civilization-altering technology. We have seen that the journey is not a simple, linear path, but a series of immense challenges and brilliant triumphs. We find ourselves today in a fascinating and pivotal moment, the NISQ era, an age of powerful but imperfect quantum machines. This is the frontier as it exists right now, a wild and noisy landscape where pioneers are learning to work with the unruly tools they have. But the true promise of the quantum age lies beyond this horizon. This final chapter is a journey into that future, an attempt to peer through the fog and glimpse the next frontier.

The primary objective that defines the next great phase of quantum computing is the quest for fault tolerance. The noisy, intermediate-scale machines of today are a crucial stepping stone, but they are ultimately a transitional technology. Their computational power is forever limited by the relentless ticking clock of decoherence. The grand prize is the creation of a fully error-corrected, fault-tolerant quantum computer. This is a machine where the fundamental unit of computation is not the fragile, noisy physical qubit, but the robust, nearly perfect logical qubit we encountered in our discussion of quantum error correction. A logical qubit is not a single particle, but a collective entity, its information cleverly encoded across the entangled state of many physical qubits. It is a system designed to be its own immune response, constantly detecting and correcting the errors that noise inevitably creates.

Achieving this will be a feat of engineering on a scale that will dwarf even the impressive accomplishments of the NISQ era. The overhead required is staggering. Current estimates for the most promising error-correcting codes, like the surface code, suggest that hundreds or even thousands of high-quality physical qubits may be required to encode a single, stable logical qubit. The path forward is therefore a dual challenge. On one front, experimentalists must continue to improve the quality of their physical qubits, pushing gate fidelities ever closer to the 99.99% mark and increasing coherence times. A small improvement in the underlying physical error rate can lead to a dramatic reduction in the overhead required for correction.

On the other front, theorists are in a race to design more efficient error-correcting codes. The surface code is a brilliant and practical design, but it is not necessarily the final word. Researchers are actively exploring new families of codes, such as Low-Density Parity-Check (LDPC) codes, which promise, on paper, to achieve the same level of protection with a much smaller number of physical qubits. The journey to fault tolerance will be a gradual one. The first milestone will be the unambiguous creation and control of a single, long-lived logical qubit. This will be followed by the challenge of performing high-fidelity gate operations between two logical qubits. From there, the goal will be to scale up, building processors with tens, then hundreds, then thousands of these stable logical qubits. It is this machine, the fault-tolerant quantum computer, that will finally unlock the full, world-changing potential of the algorithms we have discussed.

As these powerful, error-corrected machines begin to emerge, a new possibility comes into view: connecting them. The dream is not just to build a single, powerful quantum computer, but to build a global network of them, a true quantum internet. A quantum internet would be a network capable of transmitting not classical bits, but qubits themselves. It would be a system designed to generate and distribute entanglement between any two points on the globe, creating a new and powerful infrastructure for communication, computation, and sensing. The technological heart of this future network is a device known as a quantum repeater.

As we saw with Quantum Key Distribution, the signal of a single photon fades quickly in a fiber optic cable. A quantum repeater is a complex device designed to overcome this distance limitation. It works through a process called entanglement swapping. Instead of trying to send a single fragile qubit over a long distance, the repeater creates entangled pairs of particles locally and then uses a series of measurements and classical communications to "swap" the entanglement, effectively stitching together a chain of entanglement over a vast distance. Building a functional quantum repeater is a monumental challenge, requiring a delicate interplay of quantum memory, single-photon sources, and precise control, but it is the critical missing link for a global quantum network.

The applications of such a network would be transformative. Its most immediate use would be to create a foundation for provably secure communication on a global scale, making the security guarantees of QKD available between any two continents. Beyond security, a quantum internet would enable powerful new forms of distributed quantum computing. Instead of needing one massive, million-qubit processor in a single location, one could link together many smaller, less powerful quantum computers from around the world. Their combined power, connected by a fabric of shared entanglement, could be brought to bear on problems that are too large for any single machine to handle. It is the quantum equivalent of the cloud-based supercomputing clusters that are the backbone of modern scientific research.

This network could also give rise to a new generation of scientific instruments. By entangling a network of telescopes or sensors, we could create a single, continent-sized observatory with a resolution far beyond what is possible with classical technology. This could allow us to peer into the hearts of black holes or search for distant exoplanets with unprecedented clarity. The quantum internet is the vision for the next layer of our information infrastructure, a network that transmits not just data, but the spooky and powerful connections of the quantum realm itself.

The arrival of fault-tolerant hardware will also ignite a second golden age of quantum algorithm discovery. The designers of the NISQ era have been brilliant innovators, but they have been working with one hand tied behind their back, forced to design shallow circuits that can outrun the demon of noise. The freedom to design deep, complex circuits without the constant fear of decoherence will open the floodgates of possibility. We will finally be able to run Shor's algorithm on a cryptographically relevant scale, a moment that will necessitate the complete transition of our global security infrastructure to post-quantum standards. But the true excitement lies in what comes after Shor and Grover.

The availability of robust hardware will provide an experimental playground for theorists to test new algorithmic ideas that are currently confined to blackboards and academic papers. We may see the maturation of algorithms based on quantum walks, a powerful tool for analyzing complex networks and solving certain types of optimization problems. More advanced quantum simulation techniques, which are currently impractical due to their circuit depth, will become a reality, allowing for the simulation of quantum systems with a precision that far exceeds the capabilities of variational methods like VQE. This new hardware will be a powerful microscope for the world of algorithms, allowing us to discover which of our theoretical ideas hold up in practice and which new ones have yet to be imagined.

This revolution in capability will be mirrored by a revolution in usability. The programming languages and software tools of the future will look very different from the low-level circuit assembly that is common today. We will see the rise of sophisticated quantum compilers that can take a high-level description of a problem and automatically generate the most efficient, fault-tolerant sequence of gates to solve it. We will move towards a world of high-level abstraction, where a chemist or a financial analyst can use a quantum computer as a powerful accelerator without needing to be an expert in the underlying physics of CNOT and Hadamard gates.

This points to the ultimate future of computing architecture: a deeply integrated hybrid system. The future is not one where quantum computers replace our laptops and smartphones. It is a future where Quantum Processing Units (QPUs) become a standard component of our large-scale computing infrastructure, sitting alongside the CPUs and GPUs that are the workhorses of today. The data centers of tomorrow will be heterogeneous computing environments, managed by a sophisticated classical operating system that acts as a master orchestrator. When a user submits a complex computational problem, this orchestrator will intelligently decompose it, sending the parts that are best suited for sequential logic to the CPU, the parts that are good for massive parallel processing to the GPU, and the parts that are fundamentally quantum mechanical in nature to the QPU. The user may not even be aware of this complex dance; they will simply get the right answer, faster and more accurately than ever before.

This mature hybrid model will allow us to revisit the grandest ambitions of quantum machine learning. With fault-tolerant hardware, algorithms like HHL might finally become practical for certain classes of problems, potentially revolutionizing areas that rely on solving large systems of linear equations. The deeper integration of quantum accelerators with classical AI could also open up entirely new avenues of research. While the idea of a quantum computer achieving consciousness remains firmly in the realm of science fiction, it is plausible that these machines could become indispensable tools in our quest to understand intelligence itself. They might help us solve the massive optimization problems involved in training next-generation classical AI models, or they could provide insights into the nature of learning and complexity that are simply inaccessible to a classical machine.

With these mature tools in hand, the grand scientific visions we have discussed will finally come into sharp focus. In the fault-tolerant era, quantum simulation will move beyond small molecules to tackle the Everest of computational chemistry: the simulation of large, complex biomolecules like proteins and enzymes in their natural, solvated environments. This will be the dawn of a new age of rational drug design and synthetic biology, where we can engineer biological systems with atomic precision. In materials science, the design of a room-temperature superconductor will move from a theoretical dream to a concrete, computational engineering project.

The most profound applications of all may lie in the exploration of fundamental science. With a large-scale, fault-tolerant quantum computer, we will possess a tool capable of simulating the universe itself at its most extreme. Physicists will be able to build controllable models of black holes to probe the deep paradoxes that lie at the intersection of quantum mechanics and general relativity. They will be able to simulate the conditions of the early universe, just moments after the Big Bang, to understand how the fundamental forces of nature emerged from the quantum foam. There is even a tantalizing, though highly speculative, idea that spacetime itself might be an emergent property of a deeper layer of quantum entanglement. If so, a quantum computer would not just be a tool for simulating the universe; it would be a machine built in the very image of its fundamental architecture, a device that allows us to ask the deepest questions about the nature of reality itself.

This distant future will also bring our ethical and societal challenges into their most mature and urgent form. A world with a global quantum internet and quantum-powered artificial intelligence will require a new social contract. The debates we are having today about data privacy, algorithmic bias, and the governance of powerful technologies will become even more critical. A society that has access to this level of computational power will need to cultivate a new level of wisdom and foresight to wield it responsibly. We will need to build international norms and institutions capable of managing a world where the old boundaries of security and economy have been redrawn.

The journey from the first glimmer of an idea in the mind of a physicist to a globally transformative technology is a long and arduous one. The quantum age is not a single event that will arrive on a specific Tuesday. It is a gradual, unfolding process, a relentless accumulation of scientific breakthroughs, engineering triumphs, and conceptual shifts. We are living through the very first stages of that transformation, the critical period where the foundations for this new world are being laid. The path ahead is long, and the greatest challenges are still before us. But for the first time in history, the blueprint is clear, the tools are in our hands, and the next frontier of computation is no longer a distant dream. It is the tangible, thrilling, and profoundly important work of tomorrow.

* 9 7 9 8 3 1 3 9 6 2 1 3 9 *